College Degrees by Mail

100 Good Schools
that Offer Bachelor's,
Master's, Doctorates
and Law Degrees
by Home Study

John Bear, Ph.D.

Ten Speed Press

TEN SPEED PRESS
P. O. Box 7123
Berkeley, California 94707

Text and cover design by Fifth Street Design, Berkeley, California.

Library of Congress Cataloging-in-Publication Data

Bear, John, 1938 -
    College degrees by mail: 100 good schools that offer bachelor's, master's, doctorates,
and law degrees by home study / John Bear
        p. cm.
    Includes index.
    ISBN 0-89815-589-4
    1. Correspondence schools and courses—United States—Directories.
2. Degrees, Academic—United States—Directories.   I. Title.
LC901.B35 1990
374'.473—dc20   90-47097
                                                                   CIP

Printed in the United States of America

5   6   7   8   9   —   97   96   95   94   93

Dedication

For Tanya Pozerycki, diligent researcher, tireless organizer, and youngest daughter, without whose help you would not be reading this now, because the book would have come out a year later. And, as always, for Marina.

Table of Contents

Appendices

Introduction

Four Essential Facts and Assumptions

HERE ARE THE FOUR BASIC ASSUMPTIONS upon which this book is built. You already know the first, you probably know the second, you probably don't know the third, and the fourth is the reason to buy this book.

There is often no connection whatsoever between ability and degrees.

There are extremely talented and capable people who never went to college for a single day. And, as everyone knows, some of the most incompetent boobs on our planet have degrees from prestigious universities.

A degree is often more useful than a good education or valuable skills in your field.

You may be the best business manager, teacher, or pilot in three counties, but if you don't have a piece of imitation parchment that certifies you as an Associate, Bachelor, Master, or Doctor, you are somehow perceived as less worthy, and are often denied the better jobs and higher salaries that go to degree-holders, regardless of their competence.

It is easier than it ever has been to earn a degree.

Since the mid-1970s, there has been a virtual explosion in what is now called "alternative" or "nontraditional" or "external" or "off-campus" education—ways and means of getting an education, or a degree (or both, if you wish) without sitting in classrooms day after day, year after year.

But it is not always easy to find the right school.

Many of the good schools never advertise or promote themselves, either because they don't know how or because they think it unseemly. And most of the bad schools, the illegal or barely legal diploma mills, advertise all the time in national newspapers and magazines.

Let this book be your guide, your starting point, and your road map. Of course, it will require effort on your part to end up with the degree you want. I think it is safe to say that if you cannot find what you are looking for or hoping for in this book, it probably doesn't exist.

College Degrees by Mail

The Two Ideas that Make It All Possible

THERE ARE TWO VERY CLEVER IDEAS that make it possible to earn good, usable college degrees by mail. Surprisingly, both ideas have been around for a long, long time, although many people in the degree-granting business are just beginning to pay attention to them.

Idea Number One:
If you've already done it, you don't have to do it again.

When Aristotle arrived to train Alexander T. Great, it was clear to the old boy that his student *already* had learned a great deal, which did not have to be taught again, and so they could get on with the art of war and diplomacy. Compare that with many of today's students who "learn" the exports of Brazil and the parts of speech every year for eight consecutive years. As my mentor, Dr. Elizabeth Drews, wrote, "It is immoral to teach someone something he or she already knows."

Thankfully, more and more colleges and universities are giving credit for the things one already knows. If you learned a second language from your grandmother or out of a book or by living in another country, you'll still get credit for it. If you learned journalism by working on a newspaper, you'll get credit for it. If you learned meteorology while studying for your pilot's license, you'll get credit for it. That sort of thing. (How do you *get* that credit? Read on. That's what much of this book is about.)

Idea Number Two:
Meaningful learning can take place outside the classroom.

Abraham Lincoln studied law at night, by the fire. We have always known that learning can take place anywhere, any time, although for years, most universities have pretended that the only worthwhile learning, the only *degree-worthy* learning, takes place in classrooms and lecture halls. But now, more and more schools are not only acknowledging the learning that took place before you enrolled, they are making their own courses available in a multitude of ways, including

- courses by correspondence, or home study
- courses offered over cable television (or by videotape)
- courses through guided independent study, at your own pace
- courses offered over home computers linked to the university computer
- courses offered in your neighborhood, by schools that are actually located in another state or country.

Important Issues

College Degrees

What Are They?

A DEGREE IS A TITLE conferred by a school to show that a certain course of study has been successfully completed. A diploma is the actual document or certificate that is given to the student as evidence of the awarding of the degree. The following six kinds of degrees are awarded by college and universities in the United States.

The Associate's degree

The Associate's degree is a relatively recent development, reflecting the tremendous growth of two-year community colleges (which is the new and presumably more respectable name for what used to be known as junior colleges).

Since many students attend these schools for two years, but do not continue on to another school for the Bachelor's degree, a need was felt for a degree to be awarded at the end of these two years of full-time study (or their equivalent by nontraditional means). More than two thousand two-year schools now award the Associate's degree, and a small but growing number of four-year schools also award them to students who leave after two years.

The two most common Associate's degrees are the A.A. (Associate of Arts) and the A.S. (Associate of Science). But more than one hundred other titles have been devised, ranging from the A.M.E. (Associate of Mechanical Engineering) to the A.D.T. (Associate of Dance Therapy).

An Associate's degree typically requires sixty to sixty-four semester hours of credit, which, in a traditional program, normally takes two academic years (four semesters, or six quarters) to complete.

The Bachelor's degree

Most places in the world, the Bachelor's is the first university degree earned. (The Associate's is little used outside the United States.) The traditional Bachelor's degree in America is widely believed to require four years of full-time study (120 to 128 semester units), although a rather alarming report in 1990 revealed that the average time is closer to six years! But through nontraditional approaches, some people with a good deal of prior learning have earned Bachelor's degrees in as short a time as two or three months.

More than three hundred different Bachelor's degree titles have been used in the last hundred years, but the great majority of the million-plus Bachelor's degrees awarded in the United States each year are either the B.A. (Bachelor of Arts) or the B.S. (Bachelor of Science), sometimes with additional letters to indicate the field (e.g., B.S.E.E. for electrical engineering, B.A.B.A. for business administration, and so on). Other common Bachelor's degree titles include the B.B.A. (business administration), B.Mus. (music), B.Ed. (education), and B.Eng.

(engineering). Some nontraditional schools or programs award their own degrees: B.G.S. (general studies), B.I.S. (independent studies), B.L.S. (liberal studies) and so on. (Incidentally, in the late nineteenth century, educators felt that the title of "Bachelor" was inappropriate for young ladies, so some schools awarded female graduates titles such as Mistress of Arts or Maid of Science.)

The Master's degree

The traditional Master's degree requires one to two years of on-campus work after the Bachelor's. Some nontraditional Master's degrees may be earned entirely through nonresident study, while others require anywhere from a few days to a few weeks on campus.

There are several philosophical approaches to the Master's degree. Some schools regard it as a sort of advanced Bachelor's, requiring only the completion of one to two years of advanced-level studies and courses. Other schools see it as a junior Doctorate, requiring creative, original research, culminating in the writing of a thesis, or original research paper. Some programs give the student the option of choosing either approach: they may choose either to take, for example, ten courses and write a thesis, or thirteen courses with no thesis, to earn the Master's degree.

Master's degree titles tend to follow closely those of Bachelor's degrees. The M.A. (Master of Arts) and M.S. (Master of Science) are by far the most common, along with the standby of American business, the M.B.A. (Master of Business Administration). Other common Master's degrees include the M.Ed. (education), M.Eng. (engineering), M.L.S. (library science), and M.J. (either journalism or jurisprudence).

The Doctorate

The academic title of "Doctor" (as distinguished from the professional and honorary titles, to be discussed shortly) is awarded for completion of an advanced course of study, culminating in a piece of original research in one's field, known as the Doctoral thesis, or dissertation.

The total elapsed time can be anywhere from three to twelve years. The trend has been for Doctorates to take longer and longer. A typical Ph.D. now takes six or seven years, not all of it necessarily spent in residence on campus, however.

Some doctoral programs permit the use of work already done (books written, symphonies composed, business plans created, etc.) as partial (or, in a few cases, full) satisfaction of the dissertation requirement. But many schools insist on all, or almost all, new work.

The most common Doctorate is the Doctor of Philosophy (Ph.D. in North America, D.Phil. in many other countries), which need have nothing to do with philosophy. It is awarded for studies in dozens of fields, ranging from chemistry to communication to agriculture. There are more than five hundred other Doctorate titles in the English language alone. After the Ph.D., the most common include the Ed.D. (education), D.B.A. (business administration), D.P.A. (public administration), D.A. (art or administration), Eng.D. (engineering), and Psy.D.

Finally, it should be mentioned that several American schools, concerned with what one called the "Doctoral glut," are reported to be seriously considering instituting a new degree, *higher* than the Doctorate, presumably requiring more years of study and a more extensive dissertation. The name "Chancellorate" has been bandied about. Indeed, the prestigious *Chronicle of Higher Education* devoted a major article to this possibility in early 1990. It may well be that holders of a Chancellorate (Ph.C.?) would not appreciably affect the job market, since most of them will be on Social Security by the time they complete this degree.

Professional degrees

Professional degrees are earned by people who intend to enter what are often called "the professions"—medicine, dentistry, law, the ministry, and so forth. In the United States, these degrees are almost always earned *after* completing a Bachelor's degree, and almost always carry the title of "Doctor" (e.g., Doctor of Medicine, Doctor of Divinity).

In many other countries, it is common to enter professional school directly from high school, in which case the first degree earned is a Bachelor's. (For instance, there is the British Bachelor of Medicine, whose holders are invariably called "Doctor," unless they have earned the advanced degree of "Doctor of Medicine." Then they insist on being called "Mister." No one ever said the British were easy to understand.)

It is still possible to earn a law degree and many theological degrees (Doctor of Divinity, Theology, Sacred Music, etc.) through home study. Let's not even think about the consequences of attempting to teach medicine or dentistry by these methods!

Honorary degrees

The honorary degree is the stepchild of the academic world, and a most curious one at that. It has no more relationship or connection with academia than bandleader Doc Severinsen has with the world of medicine. It is, purely and simply, a title that some institutions (and some scoundrels) have chosen to bestow from time to time, and for a wide variety of reasons, upon certain people. These reasons often have to do with the donation of money, or with attracting celebrities to a commencement ceremony.

The honorary Doctorate has no academic standing whatsoever, and yet, because it carries with it the same title, "Doctor," that is used for the earned degree, it has become an extremely desirable commodity for those who covet titles and the prestige they bring. For respectable universities to award the title of "Doctor" via an honorary Doctorate is as peculiar as if the Army were to award civilians the honorary title of "General"—a title the civilians could then use in their everyday life.

More than one thousand traditional colleges and universities award honorary Doctorates (anywhere from one to fifty per year, each), and a great many Bible schools, spurious schools, and degree mills hand them out with wild abandon to almost anyone willing to pay the price. And that is why we have Doctor Michael Jackson, Doctor Ed McMahon, Doctor Frank Sinatra, Doctor Ella Fitzgerald, Doctor Mr. Rogers, Doctor Captain Kangaroo, Doctor Doctor Seuss, Doctor Jane Pauley, Dr. Bob Hope, Doctor Robert Redford, Doctor Stevie Wonder, Doctor Dan Rather, and thousands of other doctors.

Checking Out Schools

Two problems, Two Questions to Ask

A DEGREE PROGRAM IS, for many people, one of the most expensive and time-consuming things they will do in their lives. And yet some people will spend more time and energy buying a refrigerator or a television set than they will selecting a school. For such people, one of two major problems may later set in.

Problem One: The school turns out to be less than wonderful

Some people enroll in a questionable school and then, when they see their alma mater exposed on *60 Minutes* or *Inside Edition,* they wail, "But I didn't know; they had such a lovely catalog."

Problem Two: There are unpleasant surprises down the road

Some people enroll in good, legitimate schools, but then they discover, to their horror, that after three years, their Bachelor's will take *another* three years because of certain requirements they were unaware of; or that the degree title on the diploma will not be the one they expected (an anguished chap wrote me that after seven years in a program, he discovered he would be getting an M.A. in Architecture, not the Master of Architecture that he wanted); or some other dreadful situation that could have been avoided by asking enough questions in advance.

Thus there are two kinds of "checking out" to do: Will the school meet my needs? And is the school legitimate?

Question One: Will it meet my needs?

You'd think people would know this before spending thousands of dollars and years of their lives. But I have had hundreds of letters from people who received very unpleasant surprises after they had enrolled, sometimes after they had graduated. It is essential that you satisfy yourself that a given school will meet your needs before you spend any money with them. Make sure you know exactly what it will cost (no hidden "graduation fees," for instance), whether your employer will accept (and perhaps pay for) your degree, whether any relevant licensing agencies will accept the work, and so on.

Question Two: Is it legitimate?

If you have any doubts, concerns, worries, or hunches about any school, whether in this book or not, you have every right to check them out. It's a buyer's market. You can ask any questions you want about accreditation, number of students, the credentials of the people in charge, what kind of campus they have (some schools with very impressive-looking catalogs are operated from mail-forwarding services), and so on. Of course they have the right not to answer, whereupon you have the right not to enroll.

The information in this book is as complete and current as I could make it. But things change: schools change their policies, bad schools get better, good schools get worse, new schools appear, old schools disappear.

For ways and means of getting more information, see appendices A and B.

State Agencies

Some states have very tough school laws, some have very weak or almost non-existent laws, and most are somewhere in between.

Some states are very helpful and candid when someone inquires about a school in that state; others are very reluctant to say anything; and in some, it depends on who happens to receive your inquiry. Here is my current file on the appropriate agency and person in each state who is concerned with the legitimacy of schools in his or her state. (I have found that virtually all of them prefer letters to phone calls.)

Alabama
Charles Saunders, Coordinator of Private
    Schools Unit
Department of Education
348 State Office Building
Montgomery, AL 36130

Alaska
Linda Low, Director for Institutional
    Authorization
Commission on Postsecondary Education
3601 C Street, #478
Anchorage, AK 99503

Arizona
Dona Marie Markley, Director, State Board
    for Private Postsecondary Education
1812 West Monroe, #214
Phoenix, AZ 85007

Arkansas
Dr. John Spraggins, Associate Director for
    Academic Affairs
Department of Higher Education
1220 West 3rd Street
Little Rock, AR 72201

California
See information on the ever-changing
    California situation in appendix E.

Colorado
Dr. Timothy Grieder, Director, Continuing
    Education and Extended Academic
    Programs
Commission on Higher Education
Colorado Heritage Center, 2nd Floor
1300 Broadway
Denver, CO 80203

Connecticut
Dr. Donald H. Winandy, Director of
    Licensure and Accreditation
Board of Governors for Higher Education
61 Woodland Street
Hartford, CT 06105

Delaware
Dr. Ervin C. Marsh, State Supervisor,
    Certification and Personnel Division
Department of Public Instruction
Townsend Building
Box 1402
Dover, DE 19901

District of Columbia
John G. Stone III, Executive Director
Educational Institution Licensure
    Commission
605 C Street N.W., #M-102
Washington, DC 20001

Florida

Dr. C. Wayne Freeberg, Executive Director
State Board of Independent Colleges and
Universities
Department of Education
Tallahassee, FL 32399

Georgia

Dr. Janie W. Smith, Coordinator, Private
College and University Standards
Department of Education
1870 Twin Towers East
Capitol Square
Atlanta, GA 30334

Hawaii

Philip Doi, Director
Office of Consumer Protection
250 South King Street
Honolulu, HI 96813

Idaho

Eldon Nelson, Supervisor of Support Services
State Board of Education
650 West State Street
Boise, ID 83720

Illinois

Dr. Kathleen Kelly, Associate Director for
Academic and Health Affairs
Illinois Board of Higher Education
500 Reisch Building
4 West Old Capital Square
Springfield, IL 62701

Indiana

Phillip H. Roush, Commissioner
Indiana Commission on Proprietary
Education
32 East Washington Street, #804
Indianapolis, IN 46204

Iowa

Dr. Robert J. Barak, Director, Academic
Affairs and Research
Board of Regents
Lucas State Office Building
Des Moines, IA 50319

Kansas

Dr. Martine Hammond, Director of Academic
Affairs
Kansas Board of Regents
Merchants National Bank Building, 14th
Floor
Topeka, KS 66612

Kentucky

Robert Summers, Executive Director
Kentucky State Board for Proprietary
Education
P.O. Box 456
Frankfort, KY 40601

Louisiana

Dr. Larry Tremblay, Coordinator of Research
and Data Analysis
Board of Regents
161 Riverside Mall
Baton Rouge, LA 70801

Maine

Frederick Douglas, Director, Higher
Education Services
Department of Education & Cultural Services
Division of Higher Education Services
State House Station, #119
Augusta, ME 04333

Maryland

Dr. Donald Stoddard, Coordinator, Academic
Affairs
State Board for Higher Education
Jeffery Building, 16 Francis Street
Annapolis, MD 21401

Massachusetts

Dr. John Weston, Academic Program Officer,
Division of Academic Affairs
Board of Regents
1 Ashburton Place, Room 1401,
McCormack Building
Boston, MA 02108

Michigan

David Hanson, Specialist, Accreditation and
Approval
Department of Education
Higher Education Management Services
P.O. Box 30008
Lansing, MI 48909

Minnesota

Dr. E. Ann Kelly, Manager of Programs
Higher Education Coordinating Board
Suite 400, Capitol Square Building, 550
    Cedar Street
St. Paul, MN 55101

Mississippi

George Carter, Executive Secretary
Board of Trustees of State Institutions of
    Higher Learning
P.O. Box 2336
Jackson, MS 39225

Missouri

Dr. Robert Jacob, Assistant Commissioner
Coordinating Board for Higher Education
101 Adams Street
Jefferson City, MO 65101

Montana

Carrol Krause, Commissioner for Higher
    Education
Montana University System
33 South Last Chance Gulch
Helena, MT 59620

Nebraska

Sue Gordon-Gessner, Executive Director
Coordinating Commission for Postsecondary
    Education
6th Floor, Capitol Building, P.O. Box 95005
Lincoln, NE 68509

Nevada

John V. Griffin, Administrator
Commission on Postsecondary Education
1000 East William, Suite 102
Carson City, NV 89710

New Hampshire

Dr. James A. Busselle, Executive Director
Postsecondary Education Commission
2½ Beacon Street
Concord, NH 03301

New Jersey

Amorita Suarez, Director
Office of Program Review, Accreditation and
    Licensure
Department of Higher Education
225 West State Street
Trenton, NJ 08625

New Mexico

Dr. Rosalie A. Bindel, Associate Executive
    Director for Academic Affairs
Commission of Higher Education
1068 Cerillos Road
Santa Fe, NM 87501

New York

Dr. Denis F. Paul, Assistant Commissioner
Division of Academic Program Review
State Education Department
Cultural Education Center, Room 5A37
Empire State Plaza
Albany, NY 12234

North Carolina

Dr. John F. Corey, Associate Vice President
    for Planning
University of North Carolina
P.O. Box 2688
Chapel Hill, NC 27515

North Dakota

Dr. Ellen Chaffee, Associate Commissioner
    for Academic Affairs
State Board of Higher Education
State Capitol Building
Bismarck, ND 58505

Ohio

Dr. Jonathan Tafel, Director, Certificates of
    Authorization and Continuing Education
Board of Regents
30 East Broad Street, #3600
Columbus, OH 43215

Oklahoma

Dr. Melvin R. Todd, Vice Chancellor for
    Academic Administration State Regents
    for Higher Education
500 Education Building, State Capitol
    Complex
Oklahoma City, OK 73105

Oregon

Dr. David A. Young, Administrator
Office of Educational Policy and Planning
Oregon Educational Coordinating
    Commission
225 Winter Street N.E.
Salem, OR 97310

Pennsylvania
Dr. Warren D. Evans, Chief, Division of
Postsecondary Education Services
Department of Education, 9th Floor,
333 Market Street
Harrisburg, PA 17126

Rhode Island
Dr. Cynthia Ward
Associate Commissioner of Program and
Planning
Office of Higher Education
199 Promenade Street, Suite 222
Providence, RI 02908

South Carolina
Alan S. Krech, Assistant Director for
Planning and Special Projects
Commission on Higher Education
1429 Senate Street
Columbia, SC 29201

South Dakota
Roxie Thielen, Administrative Aide
Dept. of Education and Cultural Affairs
Richard Kneip Building, 700 Governors Drive
Pierre, SD 57501

Tennessee
Dr. George M. Roberts, Director of Licensure
Higher Education Commission
Parkway Towers, Suite 1900
404 James Robertson Parkway
Nashville, TN 37219

Texas
Dr. David T. Kelley, Director of Institutional
Certification
Higher Education Coordinating Board
P.O. Box 12780, Capitol Station
Austin, TX 78711

Utah
Dr. Sterling R. Provost, Assistant
Commissioner for Veterans Education
and Proprietary Schools
Utah System of Higher Education
355 West North Temple, Suite 550
Salt Lake City, UT 84180

Vermont
Ann Turkle, Executive Director
Vermont Higher Education Council
Box 70
Hyde Park, VT 05655

Virginia
Dr. John Molnar, Library Planning and
Institutional Approval Coordinator
State Council of Higher Education
101 North 14th Street, 9th Floor
Richmond, VA 23219

Washington
Elaine Jones, Policy Associate
Council for Postsecondary Education
908 East 5th Street
Olympia, WA 98504

West Virginia
Dr. Douglas Call, Director of Community
Colleges and Vocational Education
Board of Regents
P.O. Box 3368
Charleston, WV 25333

Wisconsin
David R. Stucki, Executive Secretary
State Educational Approval Board
P.O. Box 7874
Madison, WI 53707

Wyoming
Lyall Hartley, Director,
Certification/Licensure Unit
Department of Education
Hathaway Building
Cheyenne, WY 82002

Guam
William A. Kinder, Executive Director
Pacific Post-Secondary Education Council
P.O. Box 23067
G M F, Guam 96921

Puerto Rico
Ismael Ramirez-Soto, Executive Secretary
Council on Higher Education
University of Puerto Rico Station, Box F
San Juan, PR 00931

Applying to Schools

How Many Schools Should You Apply to?

There is no single answer to this question that is right for everyone. Each person will have to determine his or her own best answer. The decision should be based on the following four factors:

1. Likelihood of admission

Some schools are extremely competitive or popular and admit fewer than 10 percent of qualified applicants. Some have an "open admissions" policy and admit literally everyone who applies. Most are somewhere in between.

If your goal is to be admitted to one of the highly competitive schools (for instance, Harvard, Yale, Princeton, or Stanford), where your chances of being accepted are not high, then it is wise to apply to at least four or five schools that would be among your top choices, and to at least one "safety valve," an easier one, in case all else fails.

If you are interested in one of the good, but not world-famous, nonresident programs, your chances for acceptance are probably better than nine in ten, so you might decide to apply only to one or two.

2. Cost

There is a tremendous range of possible costs for any given degree. For instance, a respectable Ph.D. could cost around $3,000 at a good nonresident school, or more than $80,000 at a well-known university—not even taking into account the lost salary.

3. What they offer you

Shopping around for a school is a little like shopping for a new car. Many schools either have money problems or operate as profit-making businesses, and in either case, they are most eager to enroll new students. Thus it is not unreasonable to ask the schools what they can do for you. Let them know that you are a knowledgeable "shopper," and that you have this book. Do they have courses or faculty advisors in your specific field? If not, will they get them for you? How much credit will they give for prior life experience learning? How long will it take to earn the degree? Are there any scholarship or tuition reduction plans available? Does tuition have to be paid all at once, or can it be spread out over time? If factors like these are important for you, then it could pay to shop around for the best deal.

You might consider investigating at least two or three schools that appear somewhat similar, because there will surely be differences.

CAUTION: Remember that academic quality and reputation are probably the most important factors—so don't let a small financial saving be a reason to switch from a good school to a less-good school.

4. Your own time

Applying to a school can be a time-consuming process—and it costs money, too. Many schools have application fees ranging from $25 to $100. Some people get so carried away with the process of applying to school after school that they never get around to earning their degree!

Of course once you have prepared a good and detailed resume, curriculum vita, or life experience portfolio, you can use it to apply to more than one school.

Another time factor is how much of a hurry you are in. If you apply to several schools at once, the chances are good that at least one will admit you, and you can begin work promptly. If you apply to only one, and it turns you down, or you get into long delays, then it can take a month or two to go through the admission process again elsewhere.

Speeding Up the Admissions Process

The admissions process at most traditional schools is very slow; most people apply nearly a year in advance, and do not learn whether their application has been accepted for four to six months. The schools in this book will vary immensely in their policies in this regard. Some will grant conditional acceptance within a few weeks after receiving the application. ("Conditional" means that they must later verify the prior learning experiences you claim.) Others take just as long as traditional programs.

The following three factors can result in a much faster admissions process:

1. Selecting schools by admissions policy

A school's admissions policy should be stated in its catalog. Since you will find a range among schools of a few weeks to six months for a decision, the simple solution is to ask, and then apply to schools with a fast procedure.

2. Asking for speedy decisions

Some schools have formal procedures whereby you can request an early decision on your acceptance. Others do the same thing informally for those who ask. In effect what this does is put you at the top of the pile in the admissions office, so you will have the decision in, perhaps, half the usual time. Other schools use what they call a "rolling admissions" procedure, which means, in effect, that each application is considered soon after it is received instead of being held several months and considered with a large batch of others.

3. Applying pressure

As previously indicated, many schools are eager to have new students. If you make it clear to a school that you are in a hurry and that you may consider going elsewhere if you don't hear from them promptly, they will usually speed up the process. It is not unreasonable to specify a time frame. If, for instance, you are mailing in your application on September 1, you might enclose a note saying that you would like to have their decision mailed or phoned to you by October 1. (Some schools routinely telephone their acceptances, others do so if asked, some will only do so by collect call, and others will not, no matter what.)

How to Apply to a School

The basic procedure is essentially the same at all schools, traditional or nontraditional:

1. You write (or telephone) for the school's catalog, bulletin, or other literature, and admissions forms.

2. You complete the admissions forms and return them to the school, with application fee, if any.

3. You complete any other requirements the school may have (exams, transcripts, letters of recommendation, etc.).

4. The school notifies you of their decision.

It is step three that can vary tremendously from school to school. At some schools, all that is required is the admissions application. Others will require various entrance examinations to test your aptitude or knowledge level, transcripts, three or more letters of reference, a statement of financial condition, and possibly a personal interview, either on the campus or with a local representative in your area.

Happily, the majority of schools in this book have relatively simple entrance requirements. And all schools supply the materials that tell you exactly what they expect you to do in order to apply. If it is not clear, ask. If the school does not supply prompt, helpful answers, then you probably don't want to deal with them anyway. Remember, it's a buyer's market.

It is advisable, in general, *not* to send a whole bunch of stuff to a school the very first time you write to them. A short note, asking for their catalog, should suffice. You may wish to indicate your field and degree goal ("I am interested in a Master's and possibly a Doctorate in psychology") in case they have different sets of literature for different programs. It probably can do no harm to mention that you are a reader of this book; it might get you slightly prompter or more personal responses. (On the other hand, I have gotten more than a few grouchy letters from readers saying, "I told them I was a personal friend of yours, and it still took six months for an answer." Oh, dear. Well, if they hadn't said that, it might have been even longer. Or perhaps shorter. Who knows?)

The Matter of Entrance Examinations

Many nonresident degree programs, even at the Master's and Doctoral levels, do not require any entrance examinations. On the other hand, the majority of residential programs *do* require them. The main reason for this appears to be that nonresidential students do not contribute to overcrowding on the campus, so more of them can be admitted. A second reason is that nonresidential students tend to be more mature, and schools acknowledge they have the ability to decide which program is best for them.

There are, needless to say, exceptions to both reasons. If you have particular feelings about examinations—positive or negative—you will be able to find schools that meet your requirements. Do not hesitate to ask any school about their exam requirements if it is not clear from the catalog.

Bachelor's admission examinations

Most residential universities require applicants to take part or all of the ATP, or Admissions Testing Program, run by a private agency, the College Entrance Examination Board (888 7th Avenue, New York, NY 10019). The main component of the ATP is the SAT, or Scholastic Aptitude Test, which measures verbal and mathematical abilities. There are also achievement tests, testing knowledge levels in specific subject areas: biology, European history, Latin, etc. These examinations are given at centers all over North America several times each year, for modest fees, and by special arrangement in many foreign locations.

A competing private organization, ACT (American College Testing Program, P.O. Box 168, Iowa City, IA 52240), offers a similar range of entrance examinations.

The important point is that very few schools have their own exams; virtually all rely on either the ACT or the ATP.

Graduate degrees

Again, many nonresidential schools do not require any entrance examinations. When an exam is required, it is often the GRE, or Graduate Record Examination, administered by the Educational Testing Service (P.O. Box 955, Princeton, NJ 08541). The basic GRE consists of a 3½-hour aptitude test (verbal, quantitative, and analytical abilities). Some schools also require GRE subject-area exams, which are available in a variety of specific fields (chemistry, computer science, music, etc.).

Professional schools

Most law and medical schools also require a standard examination, rather than having one of their own. The MSAT (Medical School Admission Test) is given several times a year by ACT while the LSAT (Law School Admission Test) is given five times a year by ETS.

Exam preparation

There are many excellent books available at most libraries and larger bookstores on how to prepare for these various exams, complete with questions and answers. Some of these are listed in the bibliography of this book. Also, the testing agencies themselves sell literature on their tests as well as copies of previous years' examinations.

The testing agencies used to deny vigorously that either cramming or coaching could affect one's scores. In the face of overwhelming evidence to the contrary, they no longer make those claims. Some coaching services have documented score increases of 25 to 30 percent. Check the Yellow Pages or the bulletin boards on high school or college campuses.

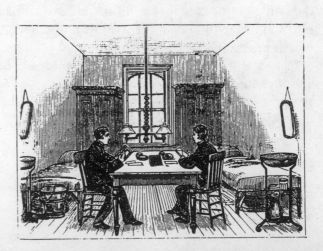

Accreditation

ACCREDITATION IS ONE OF THE MOST COMPLEX and confusing issues in higher education. It is also one of the most misused concepts—both intentionally and unintentionally. Let me try to make some sense out of the situation.

What is accreditation?

Accreditation is *not* a government process. It is a *voluntary* process that a school may go through, to obtain a stamp of approval from one of many private, non-government-affiliated accrediting associations.

It is important to know these things about accreditation:

- It is voluntary. No school is required to be accredited.
- Some very good schools (and some very bad schools) are *not* accredited.
- Some less-than-wonderful schools *are* accredited, but not many.
- There are over one hundred accrediting agencies, some legitimate, some not.
- Accreditation is a controversial topic in higher education. The last two secretaries of education have stated in no uncertain terms that the accrediting agencies are not doing their jobs, especially with respect to "nontraditional" schools such as the ones described in this book.
- More than a few schools make accreditation claims that range from confusing to misleading to downright dishonest.
- Accreditation is not the same thing as being licensed, chartered, approved, authorized, or recognized.

The importance of accreditation

Although *legitimate* accreditation is undeniably important to both schools and students (or would-be students), this importance is undermined and confused by three factors:

1. There are no national standards for accreditation. What is accreditable in New York may not be accreditable in California, and vice versa. The demands and standards of the group that accredits schools of chemistry may be very different from groups that accredit schools of forestry. And so on.

2. Many very good schools (or departments within schools) are not accredited, either by their own choice (since accreditation is a totally voluntary and often very expensive procedure), or because they are too new (all schools were unaccredited at one time in their lives), or too experimental (many would say too innovative) for the generally conservative accreditors.

3. Many very bad schools claim to be accredited—but it is always by unrecognized, sometimes nonexistent accrediting associations, often of their own creation.

Who accredits the accreditors?

There are two agencies, one private and one governmental, that have responsibility for evaluating and approving or recognizing accrediting agencies.

The Council on Postsecondary Accreditation (known as COPA) is a nationwide nonprofit corporation, formed in 1975, to evaluate accrediting associations and award recognition to those found worthy.

Within the Department of Education is the Eligibility and Agency Evaluation Staff (EAES), which is required by law to "publish a list of nationally recognized accrediting agencies which [are determined] to be reliable . . . as to the quality of training offered." This is done as one measure of eligibility for federal financial aid programs for students.

Both agencies will supply lists of accreditors they recognize. There is considerable overlap, but there are some accreditors recognized by one and not the other. In February 1993, however, things were thrown into a cocked hat when the six regional accrediting agencies announced they would be withdrawing from COPA and forming a new organization. Whether COPA will survive, and what this all means in the already confusing world of accreditation, remains to be seen.

Accreditation and the external or home study degree

One of the frequent complaints levied against the recognized accrediting agencies is that they have, in general, been slow to acknowledge the major trend to education and degrees through home study.

A few years ago, a Carnegie Commission on Higher Education analyzed the entire situation, and concluded that

> . . . as we look toward the future, it appears likely that accrediting organizations will lose their usefulness and slowly disappear. Colleges will be judged not by what some educational bureaucracy declares but by what they can do for their students. Of much greater relevance would be statistics on student satisfaction, career advancement of graduates, and data like that.

In other words, if the students at a nontraditional, nonresident university regularly produce research and dissertations that are as good as those of traditional schools or if graduates of nontraditional schools are as likely to gain admission to graduate school or high-level employment and perform satisfactorily there—then the nontraditional school is just as worthy as the traditional school.

The recognized accrediting agencies

There is one national accrediting agency and six regional accrediting associations, each with responsibility for schools in one region of the United States and its territories. Each one has the authority to accredit an entire college or university. There are also about eighty professional associations, each with authority to accredit specific departments or programs within a school. And there are at least thirty unrecognized accrediting agencies, some legitimate, most not.

Thus, it may be the case, for instance, that the North Central Association (one of the six regional associations) will accredit Dolas University. When this happens, the entire school is accredited, and all its degrees may be called accredited degrees, or more accurately, degrees from an accredited institution.

Or it may be the case that just the art department of Dolas University has been accredited by the relevant professional association, in this case the National Association of Schools of Art. If this happens, then only the art majors at Dolas U. can claim to have accredited degrees.

So if an accredited degree is important for you, the first question to ask is, "Has the school been accredited by the national accreditor or one of the six regional accreditors?" The next question is, "Has the department in which I am interested been accredited by its relevant professional association?"

There are some jobs (psychology and nursing are two examples) in which professional accreditation may be more important than regional accreditation. In other words, even if a school is accredited by its regional association, unless its psychology department is also accredited by the American Psychology Association, its degree will be less useful for psychology majors. (One of the persistent legends about accreditation has arisen because of these matters: The belief that Harvard is not accredited. Harvard University is duly accredited by its regional agency, but its psychology department—and many others—are not accredited by the relevant professional agencies.)

Each of the approved accreditors will gladly supply lists of all the schools (or departments within schools) they have accredited, and those that are candidates for accreditation. They will also answer any questions pertaining to any school's status (or lack of status) with them.

The agencies that recognize accrediting agencies

- ◆ Department of Education, Division of Eligibility and Agency Evaluation, Bureau of Postsecondary Education, Washington, DC 20202, (202) 245-9875
- ◆ Council on Postsecondary Accreditation, One Dupont Circle North, Suite 760, Washington, DC 20036, (202) 452-1433

The national accrediting agency

The only recognized agency with responsibility for schools everywhere in the U.S. is the National Home Study Council, 1601 18th Street N.W., Washington, DC 20009, (202) 234-5100. While many of the schools they accredit are vocational (truck driving, small engine repair, real estate, etc.), they are empowered to accredit academic schools offering Associates, Bachelor's, and Master's degrees, but they cannot deal with schools offering Doctorates.

The six regional accrediting agencies

There are six regional agencies, each with responsibility for dealing with all schools in the states over which they have jurisdiction.

Middle States Association of Colleges and Schools
Commission on Higher Education,
3624 Market Street
Philadelphia, PA 19104
(215) 662-5606
Delaware, District of Columbia, Maryland, New Jersey, New York, Pennsylvania, Puerto Rico, Virgin Islands.

New England Association of Schools and Colleges
15 High Street
Winchester, MA 01890
(617) 729-6762
Connecticut, Maine, Massachusetts, New Hampshire, Rhode Island, Vermont.

North Central Association of Colleges and Schools
159 Dearborn Street
Chicago, IL 60601
(800) 621-7440
Arizona, Arkansas, Colorado, Illinois, Indiana, Iowa, Kansas, Michigan, Minnesota, Missouri, Nebraska, New Mexico, North Dakota, Ohio, Oklahoma, South Dakota, West Virginia, Wisconsin, Wyoming.

Northwest Association of Schools and Colleges
7300B University Way N.E.
Seattle, WA 98105
(206) 543-0195
Alaska, Idaho, Montana, Nevada, Oregon, Utah, Washington.

Southern Association of Colleges and Schools
795 Peachtree Street N.E.
Atlanta, GA 30365
(404) 897-6125
Alabama, Florida, Georgia, Kentucky, Louisiana, Mississippi, North Carolina, South Carolina, Tennessee, Texas, Virginia.

Western Association of Schools and Colleges
Box 9990, Mills College
Oakland, CA 94613
(415) 632-5000
California, Hawaii, Guam, Trust Territory of the Pacific.

The professional accrediting agencies

There are more than eighty specialized agencies, with responsibility for accrediting programs in architecture, art, Bible education, business, chiropractic, and scores of other fields. Lists of them can be found in many standard reference books (including my own, described in appendix I), or from the two agencies that recognize accrediting agencies.

Unrecognized accrediting agencies

There are a great many accrediting agencies that are not approved or recognized either by COPA or by the Department of Education. A very small number are clearly sincere and legitimate, many others are not; none will meet the needs of a person who requires an accredited degree. Here are some of the more prominent ones:

Accrediting Commission for Specialized Colleges
The only requirement for becoming a candidate for accreditation was to mail in a check for $110.

Accrediting Commission International for Schools, Colleges and Theological Seminaries
See "International Accrediting Commission for Schools, Colleges and Theological Seminaries" in this section. After the IAC was closed down by authorities in Missouri in 1989, Dr. Reuter

retired, and turned the work over to a colleague, who juggled the words in the name and opened up one state over. All IAC schools were offered automatic accreditation by the ACI.

Alternative Institution Accrediting Association
The accreditor of several phony schools.

American Association of Accredited Colleges and Universities
An unlocatable agency, the claimed accreditor of Ben Franklin Academy.

Arizona Commission of Non-Traditional Private Postsecondary Education.
Established in the late 1970s by the proprietors of Southland University, which claimed to be a candidate for their accreditation.

Association of Career Training Schools
Their advertising to schools says: "Have your school accredited with the Association. Why? The Association Seal . . . could be worth many $ $ $ to you! It lowers sales resistance, sales costs, [and] improves image."

Commission for the Accreditation of European Non-Traditional Universities
A phony European agency.

Council for the Accreditation of Correspondence Colleges
Several questionable schools claimed their accreditation; the agency is supposed to be in Louisiana.

Council on Postsecondary Alternative Accreditation
An accreditor claimed in the literature of Western States University. Western States never responded to requests for the address of their accreditor.

Council on Postsecondary Christian Education
Unrecognized agency which accredits only schools which are a part of the World Christian Church, such as LaSalle University and Kent College of Louisiana.

International Accreditation Association
Nonexistent agency claimed by several phony schools.

International Accrediting Association
The address is the same as that of the Universal Life Church, an organization that awards Doctorates of all kinds to anyone making a "donation" of $5 to $100.

International Accrediting Commission for Schools, Colleges and Theological Seminaries
More than 150 schools were accredited by this organization. In 1989, the Attorney General of Missouri created a fictitious school, the "East Missouri Business College," which rented a one-room office in St. Louis, and issued a typewritten catalog, with such executives as "Peelsburi Doughboy" and "Wonarmmed Mann." Their marine biology text was *The Little Golden Book of Fishes*. Nonetheless, Dr. George Reuter, Director of the IAC, visited the school, accepted their money, and duly accredited them. The IAC was promptly enjoined from operating, slapped with a substantial fine, and Dr. Reuter decided to retire. (But the almost identical "Accrediting Commission International" [see above] immediately arose in Arkansas.)

International Association of Non-Traditional Schools
The claimed accreditor of several British degree mills; allegedly located in England.

International Commission for the Accreditation of Colleges and Universities
Established in Gaithersburg, Maryland, by a diploma mill called the United States University of America (now defunct) for the purpose of accrediting themselves.

Middle States Accrediting Board
A nonexistent accreditor, made up by Thomas University for the purpose of self-accreditation.

National Accreditation Association
In a mailing to schools, the NAA offered full accreditation by mail, with no on-site inspection required.

National Association for Private Post-Secondary Education
Some people have mistaken them for an accrediting agency, although they are a school information and referral service, sponsored by several schools.

National Association of Alternative Schools and Colleges
Western States University claimed in their literature that they had been accredited by this organization, which I have never been able to locate.

National Association of Open Campus Colleges
Nonexistent accreditor claimed by several phony schools.

National Association for Private Nontraditional Schools and Colleges
A serious but unrecognized effort to establish an accrediting agency specifically concerned with alternative schools and programs.

National Council of Schools and Colleges
Nonexistent accreditor claimed by a Louisiana degree mill.

West European Accrediting Society
Established from a mail forwarding service in Liederbach, West Germany, by the proprietors of a chain of diploma mills such as Loyola, Roosevelt, Lafayette, Southern California, and Oliver Cromwell Universities, for the purpose of accrediting themselves.

Western Association of Private Alternative Schools
One of several accrediting agencies claimed in the literature of Western States University. No address or phone number has ever been provided, despite many requests.

Western Association of Schools and Colleges
This is the name of the legitimate regional accreditor for California and points west. However it is also the name used by proprietors of several large diploma mills to accredit their own schools.

Western Council on Non-Traditional Private Post Secondary Education
Started by the proprietors of an Arizona school, apparently to accredit themselves.

Worldwide Accrediting Commission
Operated from a mail forwarding service in Cannes, France, for the purpose of accrediting various American-run degree mills.

Ways of Earning Credit

Correspondence Courses

YOU CAN TAKE COURSES BY MAIL from seventy-one colleges and universities in the U.S. and Canada, even though most of them don't offer degrees by mail. However the credit you earn from any of these seventy-one schools can be applied to your degree at those schools that *do* offer degrees through home study.

Each of the seventy-one institutions publishes a catalog or bulletin listing their available courses. Some offer just a few while others have hundreds. All of the schools (except the one in Canada) will accept students living anywhere in the United States, although some schools charge more for out-of-state students. About 80 percent accept foreign students, but all courses are offered only in English.

Nine of the schools offer courses at the undergraduate and graduate level, while the other sixty-two are undergraduate only.

There is a helpful directory that is, in effect, a master catalog to all seventy-one schools. It lists the course titles of every course at each school. The abbreviated one-line course titles are surprisingly informative: "Hist & phil of phys ed," "Fac career dev in schools," and ten thousand more.

The directory is called *The Independent Study Catalog,* and it is revised every few years by the publisher, Peterson's Publications (phone 800-338-3282).

Of course, you can also write directly to the schools. All of them will send you their catalog without charge. Many of the schools have popular subjects like psychology, business, and education, but some of the more esoteric topics may only be available at one or two schools, and this directory points you to them.

Correspondence courses range from one to six semester hours worth of credit, and can cost anywhere from less than $25 to more than $200 per semester hour. The average is around $60, so that a typical three-unit course would cost $180. Because of the wide range in costs, it pays to shop around.

A typical correspondence course will consist of from five to twenty lessons, each one requiring either a short written paper, answers to questions, or an unsupervised test graded by the instructor. There is almost always a supervised final examination. These can usually be taken anywhere in the world where a suitable proctor can be found (usually a high school or college teacher).

People who cannot go to a testing center, either because they are handicapped, live too far away, or are in prison, can usually arrange to have a test supervisor come to them. Schools can be extremely flexible. One correspondence program administrator told me he had two students—a husband and wife—working as missionaries on a remote island where they were the only people who could read and write. He allowed them to supervise each other.

Many schools set limits on how fast and how slow you can complete a correspondence course. The shortest time is generally two or three weeks, while the upper limit ranges from three months to two years. Some schools limit the number of courses you can take at one time, but most do not. Even those with limits are concerned only with their own institution. There is no cross-checking, and in theory one could take simultaneous courses from all seventy-one institutions.

The Seventy-one schools

Coding as follows:

✔ = one of the thirteen schools with the most college-level courses

G = school with graduate-level courses as well as undergraduate

♥ = school that welcomes students from outside the U.S.

◆ = school that prefers not to deal with foreign students but may do so

✘ = school that will not accept foreign students

Adams State College ♥
Extension Division
Alamosa, CO 81102
(303) 589-7671
Approximately 12 courses

Arizona State University ♥
Correspondence Study Office, ASB 112
Tempe, AZ 85287
(602) 965-6563
Approximately 90 courses

Athabasca University ✘
Student Services Office, Box 10000
Athabasca, Alberta, Canada T0G 2R0
(403) 645-6111
Approximately 125 courses, only for Canadians

Ball State University ✘
School of Continuing Education
Carmichael Hall
Muncie, IN 47306
(317) 285-1581
Approximately 80 courses

Brigham Young University ✔ G ♥
Independent Study, 206 Harmon Continuing
Education Building
Provo, UT 84604
(801) 378-2868
Approximately 280 courses

Central Michigan University ♥
Office of Independent Study, Rowe Hall 125
Mt. Pleasant, MI 48859
(517) 774-7140
Approximately 70 courses

Colorado State University G ♥
Correspondence Program Coordinator
C102 Rockwell Hall
Fort Collins, CO 80523
(303) 491-5288
Approximately 40 courses
Graduate courses in adult education, grantsmanship

East Tennessee State University ♥
Department of Environmental Health
P.O. Box 22960-A
Johnson City, TN 37614
(615) 929-4462
Approximately 9 courses
All courses in environmental health, rodent control, sanitation

Eastern Kentucky University ♥
Dean of Extended Programs, Perkins 217
Richmond, KY 40475
(606) 622-2001
Approximately 45 courses

Eastern Michigan University ♦
Coordinator of Independent Study
329 Goodison Hall
Ypsilanti, MI 48197
(313) 487-1081
Approximately 12 courses

Embry-Riddle Aeronautical University
Department of Independent Studies
Daytona Beach, FL 32014
(904) 239-6397
Approximately 20 courses, half in aviation subjects

Governors State University G ♥
Independent Study by Correspondence
Stuendel Road
University Park, IL 60466
(312) 534-5000, Ext. 2121
Approximately 20 courses

Home Study International ♥
6940 Carroll Avenue
Takoma Park, MD 20912
(202) 722-6572
Approximately 70 courses

Indiana State University ♥
Director of Independent Study
Alumni Center 124
Terre Haute, IN 47809
(812) 237-2555
Approximately 60 courses

Indiana University ♥
Independent Study Program, Owen Hall
Bloomington, IN 47405
(812) 335-3693
Approximately 90 courses

Louisiana State University ✔ ♥
Office of Independent Study
Baton Rouge, LA 70803
(504) 388-3171
Approximately 160 courses

Mississippi State University ♥
Continuing Education, P.O. Drawer 5247
Mississippi State, MS 39762
(601) 325-3473
Approximately 75 courses

Murray State University ♦
Center for Continuing Education
15th at Main
Murray, KY 42071
(502) 762-4159
Approximately 35 courses
Includes animal, poultry, swine, and crop science.

New York Institute of Technology ♥
American Open University, Building 66
211 Carlton Avenue
Central Islip, NY 11722
(516) 348-3300
Approximately 130 courses. Credit by examination available. Some courses available by home computer.

Ohio University ✔ ♥
Director of Independent Study
303 Tupper Hall
Athens, OH 45701
(614) 594-6721
Approximately 185 courses

Oklahoma State University ♥
Correspondence Study Department
001P Classroom Building
Stillwater, OK 74078
(405) 624-6390
Approximately 120 courses

Oregon State System of Higher Education G ♥
Office of Independent Study
Portland State University, P.O. Box 1491
Portland, OR 97207
(800) 547-8887, Ext. 4865
Approximately 100 courses

Pennsylvania State University ✔ ♥
Director of Independent Learning
128 Mitchell Building
University Park, PA 16802
(814) 865-5403
Approximately 150 courses

Purdue University ♥
Division of Media-Based Programs
116 Stewart Center
West Lafayette, IN 47907
(317) 494-7231
Approximately 8 courses
Courses in food service, pest control, pharmacology.

Roosevelt University ♥
College of Continuing Education
430 S. Michigan Avenue
Chicago, IL 60605
(312) 341-3866
Approximately 60 courses
Includes three graduate courses in psychology.

Saint Joseph's College G ♥
Continuing Education, White's Bridge Road
North Windham, ME 04062
(207) 892-6766
Approximately 50 courses

Savannah State College ♥
Correspondence Study Office, P.O. Box 20372
Savannah, GA 31404
(912) 356-2243
Approximately 25 courses

Southeastern College of the Assemblies of God ♥
Independent Study by Correspondence
1000 Longfellow Boulevard
Lakeland, FL 33801
(813) 665-4404
Approximately 40 courses, mostly in religious subjects

Southern Illinois University ♥
Division of Continuing Education
Washington Square C
Carbondale, IL 62901
(618) 536-7751
Approximately 14 courses

Southwest Texas State University ♥
Correspondence and Extension Studies
118 Medina Hall
San Marcos, TX 78666
(512) 245-2322
Approximately 40 courses

Texas Tech University G ♥
Continuing Education, P.O. Box 4110
Lubbock, TX 79409
(806) 742-1513
Approximately 90 courses

University of Alabama ✔ ♥
Independent Study Department, P.O. Box 2967
University, AL 35486
(205) 348-7642
Approximately 175 courses

University of Alaska ♥
Correspondence Study, 115 Eielson Building
403 Salcha Street
Fairbanks, AK 99701
(907) 474-7222
Approximately 65 courses

University of Arizona ♥
Continuing Education, Babcock Building
Suite 1201, 1717 E. Speedway
Tucson, AZ 85719
(602) 621-3021
Approximately 110 courses

University of Arkansas ♥
Department of Independent Study
2 University Center
Fayetteville, AR 72701
(501) 575-3647
Approximately 120 courses

University of California Extension ✔ ♥
Independent Study, 2223 Fulton Street
Berkeley, CA 94720
(415) 642-4124
Approximately 200 courses

University of Colorado ♥
Division of Continuing Education
Campus Box 178
Boulder, CO 80309
(303) 492-5145
Approximately 85 courses

University of Florida ♥
Department of Independent Study
by Correspondence
1938 West University Avenue, Room 1
Gainesville, FL 32603
(904) 392-1711
Approximately 115 courses

University of Georgia ♥
Center for Continuing Education
1197 South Lumpkin Street
Athens, GA 30602
(404) 542-3243
Approximately 130 courses

University of Idaho ♥
Correspondence Study in Idaho
Continuing Education Building, Room 116
Moscow, ID 83843
(208) 885-6641
Approximately 100 courses

University of Illinois ◆
Guided Individual Study, 1046 Illini Hall
725 S. Wright Street
Champaign, IL 61820
(217) 333-1321
Approximately 140 courses

University of Iowa ✔ G ♥
Center for Credit Programs
W400 Seashore Hall
Iowa City, IA 52242
(319) 353-4963
Approximately 140 courses

University of Kansas ♥
Independent Study
Continuing Education Building
Lawrence, KS 66045
(913) 864-4792
Approximately 120 courses

University of Kentucky ◆
Independent Studies, Frazee Hall, Room 1
Lexington, KY 40506
(606) 257-3466
Approximately 125 courses

University of Michigan ♥
Department of Independent Study
200 Hill Street
Ann Arbor, MI 48104
(313) 764-5306
Approximately 30 courses

University of Minnesota ✔ ♥
Independent Study, 45 Wesbrook Hall
77 Pleasant Street S.E.
Minneapolis, MN 55455
(612) 373-3803
Approximately 265 courses

University of Mississippi ♥
Department of Independent Study
Division of Continuing Education
University, MS 38677
(601) 232-7313
Approximately 135 courses
*Offers noncredit French and German for Ph.D.
candidates.*

University of Missouri G ♥
Center for Independent Study
400 Hitt Street
Columbia, MO 65211
(314) 882-6431
Approximately 120 courses

University of Nebraska ♥
269 Nebraska Center for Continuing Education
33rd and Holdrege
Lincoln, NE 68583
(402) 472-1926
Approximately 75 courses

University of Nevada ♥
Independent Study Department, Room 333
College Inn, 1001 S. Virginia Street
Reno, NV 89557
(702) 784-4652
Approximately 65 courses

University of New Mexico ♥
Independent Study through Correspondence
1634 University Boulevard N.E.
Albuquerque, NM 87131
(505) 277-2931
Approximately 40 courses

University of North Carolina ✔ ♥
Independent Study
201 Abernethy Hall 002A
Chapel Hill, NC 27514
(919) 962-1106
Approximately 160 courses

University of North Dakota ✘
Department of Correspondence Study
Box 8277, University Station
Grand Forks, ND 58202
(701) 777-3044
Approximately 90 courses

University of Northern Colorado G ♥
Frasier Hall, Room 11
Greeley, CO 80639
(303) 351-2944
Approximately 16 courses

University of Northern Iowa ♥
Coordinator of Credit Programs
144 Gilchrist
Cedar Falls, IA 50614
(319) 273-2121
Approximately 55 courses

University of Oklahoma ✔ ♥
Independent Study Department
1700 Asp Avenue, Room B-1
Norman, OK 73037
(405) 325-1921
Approximately 200 courses

University of South Carolina ♥
Correspondence Study
915 Gregg Street
Columbia, SC 29208
(803) 777-2188
Approximately 130 courses

University of South Dakota ♥
126 Center for Continuing Education
414 East Clark
Vermillion, SD 57069
(605) 677-5281
Approximately 95 courses

University of Southern Mississippi ♥
Department of Independent Study
P.O. Box 5056, Southern Station
Hattiesburg, MS 39406
(601) 266-4860
Approximately 90 courses

University of Tennessee ✔ ♥
Center for Extended Learning
420 Communications Building
Knoxville, TN 37996
(615) 974-5134
Approximately 180 courses
Many noncredit courses in pharmacology, creative writing, Bible study.

University of Texas ♥
Correspondence Study
Education Annex F38, P.O. Box 7700
Austin, TX 78713
(512) 471-5616
Approximately 100 courses

University of Utah ♥
Division of Continuing Education
1152 Annex Building
Salt Lake City, UT 84112
(801) 581-6485
Approximately 140 courses

University of Washington ♥
University Extension—Distance Learning
GH-23, 5001 25th Avenue N.E., Room 109
Seattle, WA 98195
(206) 543-2350
Approximately 130 courses
Many foreign language courses.

University of Wisconsin ✔ ♥
University of Wisconsin—Extension
432 North Lake Street
Madison, WI 53706
(608) 263-2055
Approximately 195 courses
Many foreign language courses.

University of Wyoming ♥
Correspondence Study Department
Box 3294, University Station
Laramie, WY 82071
(307) 766-5631
Approximately 100 courses

Utah State University ♥
Independent Study Division
Eccles Conference Center
Logan, UT 84322
(801) 750-2131
Approximately 100 courses

Washington State University ♥
Independent Study, 208 Van Doren Hall
Pullman, WA 99164
(509) 335-3557
Approximately 100 courses

Weber State College ♥
Division of Continuing Education
3750 Harrison Boulevard
Ogden, UT 84408
(801) 626-6600
Approximately 60 courses

Western Illinois University ◆
Independent Study Program, 318 Sherman Hall
West Adams Road
Macomb, IL 61455
(309) 298-2496
Approximately 70 courses

Western Michigan University ◆
Self-Instructional Programs, Ellworth Hall
Room B-102, West Michigan Avenue
Kalamazoo, MI 49008
(616) 383-0788
Approximately 75 courses

Western Oregon State College
Open Learning for the Fire Service Program
Division of Continuing Education
Monmouth, OR 97361
(503) 838-1220, Ext. 483
23 courses, more than half in fire service topics

Western Washington University ◆
Independent Study, Old Main 400
Bellingham, WA 98225
(206) 676-3320
Approximately 40 courses

Equivalency Examinations

MOST OF THE SCHOOLS IN THIS BOOK would agree that if you have knowledge of an academic field, then you should get credit for that knowledge, regardless of how or where you acquired the knowledge. The simplest and fairest way (but by no means the only way) of assessing that knowledge is through an examination.

More than two thousand colleges and universities in the United States and Canada award credit toward their Bachelor's degrees (and, in a few cases, Master's and Doctorates) solely on the basis of passing examinations, but only a handful will give most or all the credit for a degree on the basis of exams.

Many of the exams are designed to be equivalent to the final exam in a typical college class, and the assumption is that if you score high enough, you get the same amount of credit you would have gotten by taking the class—or, in some cases, a good deal more.

While there are many sources of equivalency exams, including a trend toward schools developing their own, two independent national agencies are dominant in this field. They offer exams known as CLEP and PEP.

CLEP and PEP

CLEP (the College-Level Examination Program) and PEP (the Proficiency Examination Program) administer more than seventy-five exams. They are given at hundreds of testing centers all over North America and, by special arrangement, many of them can be administered almost anywhere in the world.

CLEP is offered by the College Entrance Examination Board, known as "the College Board" (CN 6600, Princeton, NJ 08541-6600). Military personnel who want to take CLEP should see their education officer or write DANTES, CN, Princeton, NJ 08541.

PEP is offered in the state of New York by the Regents External Degree—College Proficiency Programs (Cultural Education Center, Albany, NY 12230), and everywhere else by the American College Testing Program (P.O. Box 168, Iowa City, IA 52243).

Many of the tests offered by CLEP are available in two versions: multiple-choice questions only, or multiple choice plus an essay. Some colleges require applicants to take both parts, others just the multiple choice. There are five general exams, each ninety minutes long, and multiple choice only, except English, which has the option of a forty-five-minute multiple choice and a forty-five-minute composition.

CLEP offers thirty subject-area exams, each of them ninety minutes of multiple-choice questions, with the option of an additional ninety minutes for writing an essay. The cost is around $30 per test.

PEP offers forty-three subject-area exams, most of them three hours long, but a few are four hours. The fees range from $40 to $125 per exam.

Each college or university sets its own standards for passing grades, and decides for itself how much credit to give for each exam. Both of these factors can vary substantially from school to school. For instance, the PEP test in anatomy and physiology is a three-hour multiple-choice test. Hundreds of schools give credit for passing this exam. Here, for instance, are three of them:

- ◆ Central Virginia Community College requires a score of 45 (out of 80), and awards nine credit hours for passing.
- ◆ Edinboro University in Pennsylvania requires a score of 50 to pass, and awards six credit hours for the same exam.
- ◆ Concordia College in New York requires a score of 47, but awards only three credit hours.

Similar situations prevail on most of the exams. There is no predictability or consistency within a given school. For instance, at the University of South Florida, a three-hour multiple-choice test in maternal nursing is worth eighteen units while a three-hour multiple-choice test in psychiatric nursing is worth only nine units.

So, with dozens of standard exams available, and more than two thousand schools offering credit, it pays to shop around a little and select both the school and the exams where you will get the most credit.

CLEP exams are offered in five general subject areas, which are
- ◆ Social Science and History
- ◆ English Composition
- ◆ Humanities
- ◆ Mathematics
- ◆ Natural Science

Specific-subject area exams are offered in the following fields:
- ◆ American Government
- ◆ American History I and II
- ◆ Educational Psychology
- ◆ General Psychology
- ◆ Human Growth and Development
- ◆ Introductory Marketing
- ◆ Introductory Macroeconomics
- ◆ Introductory Sociology
- ◆ Western Civilization I and II
- ◆ French I and II
- ◆ German I and II
- ◆ Spanish I and II
- ◆ American Literature
  College Composition
- ◆ Analysis and Interpretation
- ◆ English Literature
- ◆ Freshman English
- ◆ Trigonometry
- ◆ Algebra and Trigonometry
- ◆ General Biology
- ◆ General Chemistry
- ◆ Computers and Data Processing
- ◆ Introduction to Management
- ◆ Introductory Accounting
- ◆ Introductory Business Law
- ◆ Calculus and Elementary Functions
- ◆ College Algebra

PEP exams are offered in these fields:
- ◆ Abnormal Psychology
- ◆ Anatomy and Physiology
- ◆ Earth Science
- ◆ Foundations of Gerontology
- ◆ Microbiology
- ◆ Physical Geology
- ◆ Statistics
- ◆ Federal Income Taxation
- ◆ Business Policy
- ◆ Accounting I and II
- ◆ Cost Accounting
- ◆ Auditing
- ◆ Advanced Accounting
- ◆ Intermediate Business Law
- ◆ Corporate Finance
- ◆ Principles of Management
- ◆ Organizational Behavior
- ◆ Personnel Administration

- ◆ Labor Relations
- ◆ Marketing
- ◆ Management, Human Resources
- ◆ Production/Operations Management

- ◆ Fundamentals of Nursing
  (and 15 more nursing exams)
- ◆ Educational Psychology
- ◆ Reading Instruction
- ◆ Remedial Reading

How exams are scored

CLEP exams are scored on a scale of either 20 to 80 or 200 to 800. This is done to maintain the fiction that no score can have any intrinsic meaning. It is not obvious, for example, whether a score of 514 is good or bad. But any college-bound high school senior in America can tell you that 400 is pretty bad, 500 is OK, 600 is good, and 700 is great. Still, each college sets its own minimum score for which they will give credit, and in many cases all that is necessary is to be in the upper half of those taking the test.

PEP gives standard numerical or letter grades for its tests.

Anywhere from 1⅔ to 6 credits may be earned for each hour of testing. For example, the five basic CLEP tests (ninety minutes of multiple choice questions each) are worth anywhere from eight to thirty semester units, depending on the school. Thus it is possible to complete the equivalent of an entire year of college—thirty semester units—in two days, by taking and passing these five tests.

CLEP tests are given over a two-day period once each month at more than one thousand centers, most of them on college or university campuses. PEP tests are given for two consecutive days on a variable schedule in about one hundred locations, nationwide.

Persons living more than 150 miles from a test center may make special arrangements for the test to be given nearer home. There is a modest charge for this service. And for those in a big hurry, the CLEP tests are given twice each week in Washington, D.C.

There is no stigma attached to poor performance on these tests. In fact, if you wish, you may have the scores reported only to you, so that no one but you and the computer will know how you did. Then, if your scores are high enough, you can have them sent on to the schools of your choice. CLEP allows exams to be taken every six months; you can take the same PEP exam twice in any twelve-month period.

How hard are these exams?

This is, of course, an extremely subjective question. However, I have heard from a great many readers who have attempted CLEP and PEP exams, and the most common response is "Gee, that was a lot easier than I had expected." This is especially true of more mature students. The tests are designed for eighteen-to-twenty-year-olds, and there appears to be a certain amount of knowledge of facts, as well as experience in dealing with testing situations, that people acquire in ordinary life situations as they grow older.

Preparing (or cramming) for exams

The testing agencies issue detailed syllabuses describing each test and the specific content area it covers. CLEP also sells a book that gives sample questions and answers from each examination.

At least four educational publishers have produced series of books on how to prepare for such exams, often with full-length sample tests. These can be found in the reference section of any good bookstore or library.

For years, the testing agencies vigorously fought the idea of letting test-takers take copies of the test home with them. But consumer legislation in New York has made the tests available, and a good thing, too. Every so often, someone discovers an incorrect answer, or a poorly phrased question that can have more than one correct answer, necessitating a recalculation and reissuance of scores to all the thousands of people who took that test.

In recent years, there has been much controversy over the value of cramming for examinations. Many of my counseling clients have told me they were able to pass four or five CLEP exams in a row by spending an intensive few days (or weeks) cramming for them. Although the various testing agencies used to deny that cramming can be of any value, in the last few years there have been some extremely persuasive research studies that demonstrate the effectiveness of intensive studying. These data have vindicated the claims made by people and agencies that assist students in preparing for examinations. Such services are offered in a great many places, usually in the vicinity of college campuses, by graduate students and moonlighting faculty. The best place to find them is through the classified ads in campus newspapers and on bulletin boards around the campus. In forty states, the Stanley H. Kaplan Educational Centers offer preparation for dozens of different tests, ranging from college admissions to national medical boards. Although the main method of preparation involves a good deal of classroom attendance at a center (from twenty to over one hundred hours), almost all the materials can be rented for home study. (They are at 131 West 56th Street, New York, NY 10019, (212) 977-8200; outside New York, (800) 223-1782.)

Probably the best strategy is to take a sample self-scoring test from one of the various guidebooks. If you do very well, you may wish to take the real exam right away. If you do very badly, you may conclude that credit by examination is not your cup of hemlock. And if you score anywhere in between, consider cramming on your own, or with the help of a paid tutor or tutoring service.

Other examinations

Here are some other examinations that can be used to earn substantial credit toward many non-traditional degree programs.

Graduate Record Examination   The GRE is administered by the Educational Testing Service (P.O. Box 955, Princeton, NJ 08541, (212) 966-5853) and is given at nationwide locations four times each year. There is one general aptitude test and a series of advanced tests designed to test knowledge that would ordinarily be gained by a Bachelor's degree holder in a given field. The exams are available in the fields of biology, chemistry, computer science, economics, education, engineering, French, geography, geology, German, history, English literature, mathematics, music, philosophy, physics, political science, psychology, sociology, and Spanish.

Schools vary widely in how much credit they will give for each GRE. The range is from none at all to thirty semester units in the case of Regents College of the University of the State of New York.

I once met a National Guard sergeant who had crammed for, taken, and passed three GRE exams in a row, thereby earning ninety semester units in nine hours of testing. Then he took the five basic CLEP exams in two days, and earned thirty more units, which was enough to earn an accredited Bachelor's degree, start to finish, in sixteen and a half hours, starting absolutely from scratch with no college credit.

DANTES   The Defense Activity for Non-Traditional Educational Suppport, or DANTES, administers its own exams as well as CLEP and PEP exams. Once given only to active military personnel, DANTES are now available to everyone. Information available from DANTES, c/o Educational Testing Service, Mail Stop 3/X, Princeton, NJ 08541.

University End of Course Exams   Several schools offer the opportunity to earn credit for a correspondence course solely by taking (and passing) the final exam for that course. One need not be enrolled as a student in the school to do this. Two schools with especially large programs of this kind are Ohio University (Course Credit by Examination, Tupper Hall, Athens, OH 45701) and the University of North Carolina (Independent Study, Abernethy Hall 002A, Chapel Hill, NC 27514).

Advanced Placement Examinations   The College Board offers exams specifically for high-school students who wish to earn college credit while still in high school. Exams in thirteen subject areas are offered (College Board Advanced Placement Program, 888 7th Avenue, New York, NY 10106).

What if you hate exams or don't do well on them?

Don't despair. There are two other, less threatening, ways to get credit for life experience learning: special assessments and preparation of a life experience portfolio. These are discussed in the following chapter.

Credit for Life Experience Learning

THE PHILOSOPHY BEHIND CREDIT for life experience learning can be expressed very simply: Academic credit is given for what you know, without regard for how, when, or where the learning was acquired.

Consider a simple example. Quite a few colleges and universities offer credit for courses in typewriting. For instance, at Western Illinois University, Business Education 261 is a basic typing class. Anyone who takes and passes that class is given three units of credit.

Advocates of credit for life experience learning say: "If you know how to type, regardless of how and where you learned, or even if you taught yourself at the age of nine, you should still get those same three units of credit, once you demonstrate that you have the same skill level as a person who passes Business Education 261."

Of course, not all learning can be converted into college credit. But many people are surprised to discover how much of what they already know is, in fact, creditworthy. With thousands of colleges offering hundreds of thousands of courses, it is a rare subject, indeed, that someone hasn't determined to be worthy of some credit. There is no guarantee that any given school will honor any given learning experience, or even accept another school's assessment for transfer purposes. Yale might not accept typing credit. But then again, often the course title sounds much more academic than the learning experience itself, as in "Business Education" for typing, "Cross-cultural Communication" for a trip to China, or "Fundamentals of Physical Education" for golf lessons.

Eight kinds of creditworthy life experience

Here are eight major classifications of life experiences that may be worth college credits, especially in nontraditional, degree-granting programs:

1. **Work.** Many of the skills necessary in paid employment are also skills that are taught in colleges and universities. These include, for instance, typing, filing, shorthand, accounting, inventory control, financial management, map reading, military strategy, welding, computer programming or operating, editing, planning, sales, real estate appraisals, and literally thousands of other skills.

2. **Homemaking.** Home maintenance, household planning and budgeting, child raising, child psychology, education, interpersonal communication, meal planning and nutrition, gourmet cooking, and much more.

3. **Volunteer work.** Community activities, political campaigns, church activities, service organizations, volunteer work in social service agencies, hospital volunteering, and so forth.

4. Noncredit learning in formal settings. Company training courses, in-service teacher training, workshops, clinics, conferences and conventions, lectures, courses on radio or television, noncredit correspondence courses, etc.

5. Travel. Study tours (organized or informal), significant vacation and business trips, living for periods in other countries or cultures, participating in activities related to subcultures or other cultures.

6. Recreational activities and hobbies. Musical skills, aviation training and skills, acting or other work in a community theater, sports, arts and crafts, fiction and nonfiction writing, public speaking, gardening, attending plays, concerts, movies, visiting museums, designing and making clothing, and many other leisure-time activities.

7. Reading, viewing, listening. Any subject area in which a person has done extensive or intensive reading and study, and for which college credit has not been granted. This category has, for instance, included viewing various series on public television.

8. Discussions with experts. A great deal of learning can come from talking to, listening to, and working with experts, whether in ancient history, carpentry, or theology. Significant, extensive, or intensive meetings with such people may also earn credit.

The most common error people make

The most common error people make when thinking about getting credit for life experience is to confuse *time spent* with *learning*. Being a regular churchgoer for thirty years is not worth any college credit in and of itself. But the regular churchgoer who can document that he or she has prepared for and taught Sunday school classes, worked with youth groups, participated in leadership programs, organized fund-raising drives, studied Latin or Greek, taken tours to the Holy Land, or even engaged in lengthy philosophical discussions with a clergyman, is likely to get credit for those experiences. Selling insurance for twenty years is worth no credit—unless you describe and document the learning that took place in areas of marketing, banking, risk management, entrepreneurial studies, etc.

It is crucial that the experiences can be documented to the satisfaction of the school. Two people could work side by side in the same laboratory for five years. One might do little more than follow instructions in running routine experiments, setting up and dismantling apparatus, and then head home. The other, with the same job title, might do extensive reading in the background of the work being done, get into discussions with supervisors, make plans and recommendations for other ways of doing the work, propose or design new kinds of apparatus, or develop hypotheses on why the results were turning out the way they were.

It is not enough just to say what you did, or to submit a short resume. The details and specifics must be documented. The two most common ways this is done are by preparing a life experience portfolio (essentially a long, well-documented, annotated resumé), or by taking an equivalency examination to demonstrate knowledge gained.

Presenting your learning: The life experience portfolio

Most schools that give credit for life experience learning require that a formal presentation be made, usually in the form of a life experience portfolio. Each school will have its own standards for the form and content of such a portfolio, and many, in fact, offer either guidelines or courses (some for credit, some not) to help the nontraditional student prepare the portfolio.

Several books on this subject have been published by the Council for Adult and Experiential Learning, 223 West Jackson Boulevard, #570, Chicago, IL 60606, phone (312) 922-5909.

CAEL also offers a set of sample portfolios. The cost is $65 for introductory materials plus four large sample portfolios, or $80 for nine portfolios, representing seven schools. This is the sort of thing that it may be worth trying to convince a local public or community college library to acquire.

The University of the State of New York offers a most helpful guide called the *Self-Assessment and Planning Manual*, specifically geared to their Regents College programs, but useful anywhere. The cost is $12, including postage, from Regents College, Cultural Education Center, SD45, Albany, NY 12230.

Here are twenty-four other means by which people have documented life experience learning, sometimes as part of a portfolio, sometimes, not:

- official commendations
- audiotapes
- slides
- course outlines
- bills of sale
- exhibitions
- programs of recitals and performances
- videotapes
- awards and honors
- mementos
- copies of speeches made
- licenses (pilot, real estate, etc.)

- certificates
- testimonials and endorsements
- interviews with others
- newspaper articles
- official job descriptions
- copies of exams taken
- military records
- samples of arts or crafts made
- samples of writing
- designs and blueprints
- works of art
- films and photographs

How life experience is turned into academic credit

It isn't easy. In a perfect world, there would be universally accepted standards, by which it would be as easy to measure the credit value in a seminar on refrigeration engineering as it is to measure the temperature inside a refrigerator. Indeed, some schools and national organizations are striving toward the creation of extensive "menus" of nontraditional experiences, such that anyone doing the same thing would get the same credit.

There continues to be progress in this direction. Many schools have come to agree, for instance, on aviation experience: a private pilot's license is worth four semester units; an instrument rating is worth six additional units; and so forth.

The American Council on Education, a private organization, regularly publishes a massive multivolume set of books, in two series: *The National Guide to Educational Credit for Training Programs* and *Guide to the Evaluation of Educational Experiences in the Armed Forces*.

Many schools use these volumes to assign credit directly, and others use them as guidelines in doing their own evaluation. A few examples will demonstrate the sort of thing that is done:

- The Red Cross nine-day training course in The Art of Helping is evaluated as worth two semester hours of social work.

- The John Hancock Mutual Life Insurance Company's internal course in technical skills for managers is worth three semester hours of business administration.
- Portland Cement Company's five-day training program in kiln optimization, whatever that may be, is worth one semester hour.
- The Professional Insurance Agents' three-week course in basic insurance is worth six semester units: three in principles of insurance and three in property and liability contract analysis.
- The army's twenty-seven-week course in ground surveillance radar repair is worth fifteen semester hours: ten of electronics and five of electrical laboratory.
- The army legal clerk training course can be worth twenty-four semester hours, including three in English, three in business law, three in management, etc.

There are hundreds of additional business and military courses that have been evaluated already, and thousands more that will be worth credit for those who have taken them, whether or not they appear in these A.C.E. volumes.

Some inspiration

There are always some people who say, "Oh, I haven't ever done anything worthy of college credit." I have yet to meet anyone with an IQ higher than room temperature who has not done at least some creditworthy things, assuming they were presented properly in a portfolio. Just to inspire you, then, here is a list of one hundred things that *could* be worth credit for life experience learning. The list could easily be ten or one hundred times as long.

- Playing tennis
- Preparing for natural childbirth
- Leading a church group
- Taking a body-building class
- Speaking French
- Selling real estate
- Studying gourmet cooking
- Reading *War and Peace*
- Building model airplanes
- Touring through Belgium
- Learning shorthand
- Starting a small business
- Navigating a small boat
- Writing a book
- Buying a Persian carpet
- Watching public television
- Decorating a home or office
- Attending a convention
- Being a counselor at camp
- Studying Spanish
- Bicycling across Greece
- Interviewing senior citizens
- Living in another culture
- Writing advertisements
- Throwing a pot
- Repairing a car
- Performing magic
- Attending art films
- Welding and soldering
- Designing and weaving a rug
- Negotiating a contract
- Editing a manuscript
- Planning a trip
- Steering a ship
- Appraising an antique
- Writing a speech
- Studying first aid or C.P.R.
- Organizing a union
- Researching international laws
- Listening to Shakespeare's plays on tape
- Designing a playground
- Planning a garden
- Devising a marketing strategy
- Reading the newspaper
- Designing a home
- Attending a seminar
- Playing the piano
- Studying a new religion
- Visiting Civil War battlegrounds
- Taking ballet lessons
- Helping a dyslexic child
- Riding a horse

- Pressing flowers
- Keeping tropical fish
- Writing public relations releases
- Writing for the local newspaper
- Running the P.T.A.
- Acting in a community theater
- Flying an airplane
- Designing a quilt
- Taking photographs
- Building a table
- Developing an inventory system
- Programming a home computer
- Helping in a political campaign
- Playing a musical instrument
- Painting a picture
- Playing political board games
- Serving on a jury
- Volunteering at the hospital
- Visiting a museum
- Attending a "great books" group
- Sewing and designing clothes
- Playing golf
- Having intensive talks with a doctor
- Teaching the banjo

- Reading the Bible
- Leading a platoon
- Learning Braille
- Operating a printing press
- Eating in an exotic restaurant
- Running a store
- Planning a balanced diet
- Reading *All and Everything*
- Learning sign language of the deaf
- Teaching Sunday School
- Training an apprentice
- Being an apprentice
- Hooking a rug
- Learning yoga
- Laying bricks
- Making a speech
- Being Dungeonmaster
- Negotiating a merger
- Developing film
- Learning calligraphy
- Applying statistics to gambling
- Doing circle dancing
- Taking care of sick animals
- Reading this book

The matter of special assessments

There is a middle ground between taking an exam and preparing a portfolio. For people whose knowledge is both extensive and in an uncommon field (or at least one for which no exams have been developed), some schools are willing to conduct special assessments for a single student. At the University of the State of New York, both for its students and for Regents Credit Bank depositors (see the section on the Credit Bank), this takes the form of an oral examination. They will find at least two experts in your field, be it Persian military history, paleontology, French poetry, or whatever. Following a three-hour oral exam, conducted at everyone's mutual convenience in Albany, New York, the examiners decide how many credits to award for that particular knowledge area.

Credit for Foreign Academic Experience

THERE ARE MANY THOUSANDS of universities, colleges, technical schools, institutes, and vocational schools all over the world whose courses are at least the equivalent of work at American universities. In principle, most universities are willing to give credit for work done at schools in other countries.

But can you imagine the task of an admissions officer faced with the student who presents an Advanced Diploma from the Wysza Szkola Inzynierska in Poland, or the degree of Gakushi from the Matsuyama Shoka Daigaku in Japan? Are these equivalent to a high school diploma, a Doctorate, or something in between?

Until 1974, the U.S. Office of Education offered the service of evaluating educational credentials earned outside the United States and translating them into approximately comparable levels of U.S. achievement. This service is no longer available from the government which has chosen, instead, to recognize some private nonprofit organizations who perform the evaluation service.

These services are used mostly by the schools themselves to evaluate applicants from abroad, or with foreign credentials, but individuals may deal with them directly, at relatively low cost.

The costs run from $60 to $150 or more, depending on the complexity of the evaluation. Some of the services are willing to deal with non-school-based experiential learning as well. The services operate quickly; less than two weeks for an evaluation is not unusual. While many schools will accept the recommendations of these services, others will not. Some schools do their own foreign evaluations.

It may be wise, therefore, to determine whether a school or schools in which you have interest will accept the recommendations of such services before you invest in them.

Typical reports from the services will give the exact U.S. equivalents of non-U.S. work, both in terms of semester units earned, and of any degrees or certificates earned. For instance, they would report that the Japanese degree of Gakushi is almost exactly equivalent to the American Bachelor's degree.

Organizations performing these services include:

Credentials Evaluation Service
P.O. Box 24040, Los Angeles, CA 90024 (213) 475-2133

Educational Credential Evaluators, Inc.
P.O. Box 17499, Milwaukee, WI 53217 (414) 964-0477

International Consultants of Delaware, Inc.
109 Barksdale Professional Center, Newark, DE 19711 (302) 737-8715
or
P.O. Box 5399, Los Alamitos, CA 90721 (213) 430-2405

Educational International
50 Morningside Drive, New York, NY 10025 (212) 662-1768

International Education Research Foundation
P.O. Box 66940, Los Angeles, CA 90066 (213) 390-6276

World Education Services
P.O. Box 745, Old Chelsea Station, New York, NY 10011 (212) 460-5644

The Credit Bank Service

MANY PEOPLE HAVE VERY COMPLICATED educational histories. They may have taken classes at several different universities and colleges, some evening or summer school classes, perhaps some company-sponsored seminars, some military training classes, and possibly a whole raft of other, informal learning experiences. They may have credits or degrees from schools that have gone out of business, or whose records were destroyed in a war or fire. When it comes time to present their educational past, it may mean assembling dozens of diverse transcripts, certificates, diplomas, job descriptions, and the like, often into a rather large and unwieldy package.

There is, happily, an ideal solution to these problems: the Regents Credit Bank, operated by the enlightened Department of Education of the state of New York, and available to people anywhere in the world.

The Regents Credit Bank is an evaluation and transcript service for people who wish to consolidate their academic records, perhaps adding credit for nonacademic career and learning experiences (primarily through equivalency examinations). The Credit Bank issues a single, widely accepted transcript on which all credit is listed in a simple, straightforward, and comprehensible form.

The Credit Bank works like a money bank, except you deposit academic credits, as they are earned, whether through local courses, correspondence courses, equivalency exams, and so forth.

Seven kinds of deposits that can be made

There are seven basic categories of learning experiences that can qualify to be "deposited" in a Credit Bank account, and of course various elements of these seven can be combined as well:

1. College courses taken either in residence or by correspondence from regionally accredited schools in the U.S., or their equivalent in other countries.

2. Scores earned on a wide range of equivalency tests, either civilian or military.

3. Military service schools and military occupational specialties that have been evaluated for credit by the American Council on Education, as described earlier.

4. Noncollege learning experiences, offered as company courses, seminars, or in-house training from many large and smaller corporations, and evaluated by the American Council on Education or the New York National Program on Noncollegiate Sponsored Instruction.

5. Pilot training licenses and certificates issued by the Federal Aviation Administration.

6. Approved nursing performance examinations.

7. Special assessment of knowledge gained from experience or independent study.

The first six of these have predetermined amounts of credit. The CLEP basic science exam will always be worth six semester units. Fluency in Spanish will always be worth twenty-four semester units. Xerox Corporation's course in repair of the 9400 copier will always be worth two semester units. The Army course in becoming a bandleader will always be worth twelve semester units. And so forth, for thousands of already-evaluated nonschool learning experiences.

The seventh category can be extremely flexible and variable. Special assessment is a means of earning credit for things learned in the course of ordinary living or job experience. The Credit Bank assesses this learning by appointing a panel of two or more experts in the field. Except in rare cases, it is necessary to go to Albany, New York, to meet with this panel.

The panel may wish to conduct an oral, a written, or, in the case of performers, a performance examination. They may wish to inspect a portfolio of writing, art, or documentation. Following the evaluation, whatever form it may take, the panel makes its recommendations for the amount of credit to be given. This has, in practice, ranged from zero to more than eighty semester units, although the typical range for each separate assessment is probably from fifteen to thirty credits.

The Credit Bank has, for example, conducted special assessments in journalism, ceramics, Hebrew language, electronics engineering, aircraft repair and maintenance, and Japanese culture studies, among many others.

There is a relatively modest fee ($250 at this writing) to set up a Credit Bank account, which includes evaluation of prior work (except special assessments), and one year of update service. After the first year, there is a fee each time a new "deposit" of credits is made.

Work that is, for whatever reason, deemed not creditworthy may still be listed on the transcript as "noncredit work." Further, the Credit Bank will only list those traditional courses from other schools that the depositor wishes included. Thus any previous academic failures, low grades, or other embarrassments may be omitted from the Credit Bank report.

Students who enroll in the Regents College of the University of the State of New York automatically get Credit Bank service, and do not need to enroll separately.

The address is Regents Credit Bank, Regents College, University of the State of New York, 1450 Western Avenue, Albany, NY 12230.

One Hundred Good Schools Offering Degrees Entirely or Almost Entirely by Home Study

INFORMATION ON ONE HUNDRED SCHOOLS (or one hundred and thirteen, to be exact) follows, on the next one hundred and thirteen pages. I think it is self-explanatory.

The one important thing to bear in mind is that things change. People usually don't think of something like a university moving (but they do), or going out of business (a major college or university goes out of business at least once a month, on the average), or changing its phone numbers (all the time!), or even changing its name (like College of New Jersey becoming Princeton, Kings College becoming Columbia, Queens College becoming Rutgers, and hundreds of other examples).

If a school is listed in the next hundred pages but you can't get in touch with them, see appendix A.

If a school is not listed in the next hundred pages, and you want to know about them, see appendix B.

Adam Smith University

Unaccredited nonresident Bachelor's and Master's degrees in many fields.

5000A West Esplanade, #215
Metairie, LA 70006

Telephone: (504) 837-3010
Fax: ——

Toll-free phone: (800) 732-3796
Year established: 1991

Degree levels available: Bachelor's, Master's
Key person: Dr. Donald Grunewald, President
Accreditation: Unaccredited
Residency: Nonresident
Ownership status: Proprietary
Cost index: $$*

Fields of study or special interest:
Many fields

Other information:
No new teaching is done. Degrees are based on assessment of work done at accredited schools elsewhere, and on life experience and independent study. President Grunewald has his Doctorate from Harvard, is former president of Mercy College, and lives in New York.

Honorary doctorates may be conferred.

*Tuition costs change so often, and have so many variable and individual factors for each student, that it is impossible to provide specific costs for every degree. Each school listing has from one ($) to five ($$$$$) dollar signs, whose meaning is as follows. The cost estimates are for a complete degree program, not for one semester or one year.

$	One of the least expensive schools of its kind, generally from $0 to $2,000.
$$	A lower-priced school, typically from $2,000 to $5,000.
$$$	An average-priced school, typically from $5,000 to $10,000.
$$$$	A higher-priced school, typically from $10,000 to $15,000.
$$$$$	One of the more expensive schools, typically from $15,000 and up.

American College

Accredited degrees and credentials for life insurance people and financial consultants through distance learning plus two weeks residency in Pennsylvania.

270 Bryn Mawr Avenue
Bryn Mawr, PA 19010

Telephone: (215) 526-1000   Toll-free phone: ——
Fax: (215) 526-1310   Year founded: 1927

Key person: Shirley P. Steinman, CLU, ChFC
Degree levels: Master's
Accreditation: Accredited
Residency status: Short residency
Ownership status: Nonprofit, independent
Cost index: $$

Fields of study or special interest:
Professional

Other information:
American offers an external Master of Science in financial services and Master of Science in management program, through a combination of distance learning courses and two one-week residency programs. Also offers the Chartered Life Underwriter (CLU) and Chartered Financial Consultant (CFC) designation programs. Courses are developed by resident faculty, and taken by students around the world. Students study independently or in classes which are sponsored by local CLU and CFC chapters as well as by other universities and professional associations. Examinations are given by computer wherever possible.

The college operates an office of student services with counselors available on weekends to answer questions and give advice by phone. The purpose is to eliminate some of the problems that arise in distance education by providing a stronger student/college relationship.

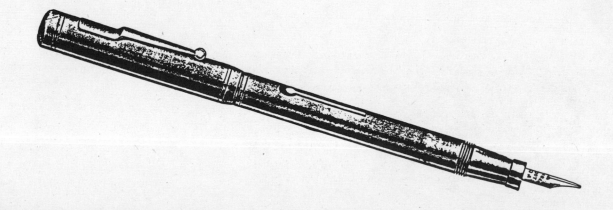

American University of London

Unaccredited nonresident degrees at all levels through an Iowa-registered school located in England.

Archway Central Hall, Archway Close
London, N19 3TD England

Telephone: (44-71) 263-2986   **Toll-free phone:** ——
Fax: (44-71) 281-2815   **Year established:** 1984

Degree levels: Bachelor's, Master's, Doctorate
Key person: Khurshid A. Khan, Ph.D.
Accreditation: Unaccredited
Ownership status: Nonprofit, independent
Residency: Nonresident
Cost index: $$$ (residential), $$ (nonresidential)

Fields of study or special interest:
Liberal arts, business, engineering, sciences

Other information:
The University operates under the laws of the State of Iowa (which registers, but does not investigate schools). Originally established as the London College of Science and Technology in 1984, the name was changed in 1986. Resident (full-time) Bachelor's, Master's, and Ph.D. programs are offered in London. The literature states that AUL undergraduate credits are accepted for transfer at many accredited U.S. schools. Resident B.B.A, B.S., M.B.A., and M.S. courses are also offered through eight affiliated colleges in London, Abu-Dhabi, Canada, Saudi Arabia, and Pakistan. Nonresident (external) degree programs at all levels are offered through the Distance Learning Center. Credit is earned through independent study, prior work, examination, and courses offered by the armed forces. Each student works under one or more adjunct faculty through guided independent study and research. A thesis and examination is required of Master's (one year) and Ph.D. (two years) candidates. Students with prior credit may apply for "transfer student" status.

Antioch University

Accredited M.A. in many fields from one of the pioneers in U.S. higher education. Degrees require a total of two five-day seminars on campus.

Individualized Master of Arts Program
800 Livermore Street
Yellow Springs, OH 45387

Telephone: (513) 767-6325
Fax: (513) 767-1891

Toll-free phone: ——
Year established: 1852

Degree levels: Master's
Key person: Michael Anderson, Registrar
Accreditation: Accredited
Ownership status: Nonprofit, independent
Residency: Short residency
Cost index: $$$$

Fields of study or special interest:
Many fields

Other information:
Student-designed programs leading to the Master of Arts degree; requires two five-day seminars on Antioch's Yellow Springs, Ohio campus. Students develop individualized curricula under the direction of two degree committee members who are recruited by the student and approved by Antioch University, then complete the coursework in their own community. Coursework may include independent study, research, practicums, workshops, conferences, tutorials, and traditional courses at other institutions. A thesis is required. Popular fields include conflict resolution, peace studies, counseling, applied psychology, creative writing, environmental studies, women's studies, and education. Antioch also offers educational programs through campuses in Los Angeles, Santa Barbara, Seattle, Keene, New Hampshire, and other locations worldwide.

:habasca University

More than 10,000 Canadians are earning accredited Bachelor's degrees through this school's sophisticated home study programs.

Box 10,000
Athabasca, Alberta TOG 2RO Canada

Telephone: (403) 675-6168
Fax: ——

Toll-free phone: ——
Year established: 1970

Degree levels: Bachelor's
Key person: Michael Neville
Accreditation: Accredited
Ownership status: Nonprofit, independent
Residency: Nonresident
Cost index: $$

Fields of study or special interest:
Many fields

Other information:
An open distance-education institution serving more than 10,000 students across Canada. (Only Canadian residents or foreigners resident in Canada are accepted.) Bachelor's degrees in administration, arts, general studies, English, history, sociology/anthropology, psychology, Canadian studies, information systems, and French. All distance education courses are offered through sophisticated home study packages. Students set up their own study schedules and work at their own pace. There are six degree programs: Bachelor of Administration, Bachelor of Arts, Bachelor of Commerce, Bachelor of General Studies, Bachelor of Nursing, and Bachelor of Science. All students are assigned a telephone tutor to whom they have toll-free access. Some courses are supplemented by radio and television programs, audio- and videocassettes, seminars, laboratories, or teleconference sessions.

Atlantic Union College

Accredited Bachelor's degree can be earned in many fields of study with four weeks on campus.

Adult Degree Program
P.O. Box 1000
South Lancaster, MA 01561

Telephone: (508) 368-2000
Fax: (508) 368-2015

Toll-free phone: (800) 282-2030
Year established: 1882

Degree levels: Bachelor's
Key person: Ottilie Stafford
Accreditation: Accredited
Ownership status: Nonprofit, church
Residency: Short residency
Cost index: $$

Fields of study or special interest:
Many fields

Other information:
Students take one "unit" each semester. A "unit" is a six-month study project, requiring two weeks on campus, and the balance of the time in independent study. A minimum of at least the two final units must be taken within the Adult Degree Program; hence four weeks of residency is required to earn the Bachelor's degree. Bachelor's degrees are offered in art, behavioral science, communications, computer science, education, English, history, interior design, modern languages, personal ministries, physical education, psychology, regional studies, religion, theology, and women's studies. Experiential learning credit can be earned through portfolio appraisal.

Brigham Young University

Accredited Bachelor of Independent Studies is done through home study plus short periods of on-campus seminars.

305 Harman Building
Provo, UT 84602

Telephone: (801) 378-4351
Fax: (801) 378-5278

Toll-free phone: ——
Year established: 1875

Degree levels: Bachelor's
Key person: Dr. Robert W. Spencer
Accreditation: Accredited
Ownership status: Nonprofit, private
Residency: Short residency
Cost index: $$

Fields of study or special interest:
Independent studies

Other information:
The Bachelor of Independent Studies degree program involves independent study and a short period of on-campus study. The degree requires attendance at a maximum of five two-week seminars on campus, one for each of five areas of study. Students who have earned 32 or more semester hours of accepted college credit within the past 10 years may transfer those credits into the program. Only one study area may be waived by CLEP exam, and only with a score of 610 or higher.

British Columbia Open University

Accredited nonresident Bachelor's degrees in many fields for Canadian citizens.

Box 94000
Richmond, BC V6Y 2A2 Canada

Telephone: (604) 660-2221
Fax: ——

Toll-free phone: (800) 663-9711
Year established: 1978

Degree levels: Bachelor's
Key person: Ian Mugridge
Accreditation: Accredited
Ownership status: Nonprofit, state
Residency: Nonresident
Cost index: $

Fields of study or special interest:

Administrative studies, applied science and natural resources, arts, education, health science, human services, science, biology, economics, geography, history, mathematics, psychology and sociology

Other information:

The program is only available to Canadian citizens. The university is part of the Open Learning Agency of British Columbia. It administers a provincial credit bank and offers collaborative programs in such areas as fine art, music therapy, and health science with other provincial institutions. The credit bank allows students to accumulate credit for previous college courses, other courses and programs, and experiential learning.

A course package is sent to each student at beginning of the course. It includes a course manual, textbooks, and assignments. It may also include audio- or videocassettes, lab kits, or software (for some courses student must have access to a computer). For some courses, support programs are broadcast on the Knowledge Network television channel. At the end of most courses a final exam is given at exam centers throughout Canada.

BCOU offers three types of degree programs. The Major Program requires specialization in one area, and classroom study may be required to complete the degree. The General Program requires lower level of specialization in two areas. General Studies allows student to choose as much or little specialization as desired. In the latter two methods, work is done through "open study" at a distance. For every course, the student is assigned a tutor. Tutors have regularly scheduled telephone consultation hours. The university also offers graduate-level courses, but no graduate degree program.

Burlington College

Accredited Bachelor's degree in various liberal arts fields requires four days on campus each semester for a minimum of two semesters.

95 North Avenue
Burlington, VT 05401

Telephone: (802) 862-9616
Fax: ——

Toll-free phone: ——
Year established: 1972

Degree levels: Bachelor's
Key person: Larry Lewak
Accreditation: Accredited
Ownership status: Nonprofit, independent
Residency: Short residency
Cost index: $$$

Fields of study or special interest:
Liberal arts and humanities

Other information:
Bachelor of Arts through the "Independent Degree Program" (IDP), primarily through nonresident study. IDP students must have completed 60 college credits and have "strong writing skills and a track record in independent study," and must be able to spend four days on the Vermont campus at the beginning of each semester. IDP students must complete a minimum of 30 credits through the program, regardless of prior experience. Although programs are highly individualized, the school specifically encourages applicants whose interests fall in the fields of fine arts, feminist studies, humanities, psychology, transpersonal psychology, or "almost any liberal arts area(s) of study."

Caldwell College

Accredited Bachelor's degrees in many fields with only four days a year on campus.

External Degree Program
9 Ryerson Avenue
Caldwell, NJ 07006

Telephone: (201) 228-4424
Fax: (201) 228-2897

Toll-free phone: ——
Year established: 1939

Degree levels: Bachelor's
Key person: Marilyn S. Goodson
Accreditation: Accredited
Ownership status: Nonprofit, church
Residency: Short residency
Cost index: $$$

Fields of study or special interest:
Many fields

Other information:
Bachelor's degrees in business administration, English, foreign languages, history, psychology, religious studies, and sociology. This is primarily an off-campus, independent study program which utilizes tutorial relationships wuth professors.

Students spend one weekend per semester on campus. Credit is given for life experience assessment and by examination.

California Coast University

Unaccredited Bachelor's, Master's and Doctorates in administration, engineering, education and behavioral sciences entirely through home study.

700 North Main Street
Santa Ana, CA 92701

Telephone: (714) 547-9625   Toll-free phone: (800) 854-8768
Fax: ——   Year established: 1972

Degree levels: Bachelor's, Master's, Doctorates
Key person: Dr. Thomas M. Neal, Jr.
Accreditation: Unaccredited
Ownership status: Proprietary
Residency: Nonresident
Cost index: $$$

Fields of study or special interest:
Administration and management, engineering, behavioral science, and education

Other information:
California Coast University was one of the first of California's nontraditional, nonresident universities. Credit is given for prior achievements and experience. Students may request "credit by experiential learning," and/or may be given the opportunity to take a challenge examination prepared and administered by the university.

Each student is assigned a faculty advisor who guides in development of individualized study program. Each study program includes independent study as well as additional testing, writing, and research if necessary. Every student develops a proposal for a topic to study which is appropriate for his or her major and degree level, and writes a research project (or thesis or dissertation).

All department heads and adjunct faculty hold degrees from traditional schools. The university operates from its own building in a Los Angeles suburb, and maintains a lending library to ensure availability of textbooks for all students throughout the world. California Coast is accredited by the National Association for Private Nontraditional Schools and Colleges, a legitimate but unrecognized accrediting agency which is applying for recognition from the Department of Education. Original name: California Western University.

California College for Health Sciences

Accredited Associate's, Bachelor's and Master's degrees in the health sciences entirely through correspondence study plus locally given exams.

222 West 24th Street
National City, CA 91950

Telephone: (619) 477-4800
Fax: (619) 477-4360

Toll-free phone: (800) 221-7374
Year established: 1979

Degree levels: Associate's, Bachelor's, Master's
Key person: Judith Eberhart
Accreditation: Accredited
Residency: Nonresident
Cost index: $$

Fields of study or special interest:
Health services

Other information:
Bachelor of Science in health sciences management and Master of Science in community health administration and wellness promotion, entirely through home-study courses. Any course may be challenged by taking the final exam without taking the course. The program prepares health professionals to become health promotion specialists working in private industry or education. Nondegree programs are offered in wellness management, wellness program development, and wellness counseling.

The Master's program is designed particularly for those already employed in a health care setting. The core of the program is a series of correspondence courses. Texts and syllabuses are mailed to students, who complete assignments, mail them in, and have comments and corrections mailed back by the faculty. Students are expected to complete one credit per month, so that a three-credit course should take three months, and normally *must* be completed within six months. Exams must be supervised by an approved proctor, and may be taken anywhere.

The school is accredited by the National Home Study Council, a recognized accreditor.

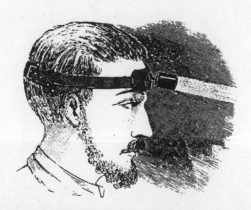

California Pacific University

Unaccredited Bachelor's, Master's and Doctorates in business and management areas entirely by correspondence study.

10650 Treena Street #203
San Diego, CA 92131

Telephone: (619) 695-3292
Fax: ——

Toll-free phone: ——
Year established: 1976

Degree levels: Bachelor's, Master's, Doctorate
Key person: N. C. Dalton, Ph.D.
Accreditation: Unaccredited
Ownership status: Nonprofit, private
Residency: Nonresident
Cost index: $$

Fields of study or special interest:
Business, management, and human behavior

Other information:
Bachelor's, Master's, and Doctorate in business administration, and M.A. in management or human behavior, entirely by correspondence study using the school's "highly structured programs." Limited experiential credit is given at undergraduate level only. Students are supplied with study guides written by university faculty, to accompany recognized textbooks in the field.

The school is "committed to the training and education of business managers and leaders in the technical, quantitative, and theoretical areas of business management, without neglecting the all important human side of business enterprise."

California State University, Dominguez Hills

Accredited Master of Arts in philosophy, music, art, history, or literature from a state university entirely through home study.

SAC 2/ Room 2126
1000 East Victoria Street
Carson, CA 90747

Telephone: (213) 516-3743
Fax: (213) 516-3449

Toll-free phone: ——
Year established: 1960

Degree levels: Master's
Key person: Dr. Arthur L. Harshman
Accreditation: Accredited
Ownership status: Nonprofit, state
Residency: Nonresident
Cost index: $$

Fields of study or special interest:
Humanities (philosophy, music, art, history, and/or literature)

Other information:
The Master of Arts can be earned entirely through home study, primarily through a method called "parallel instruction" in which the student at home does pretty much the same thing as residential students do, in the same time frame. They simply do not attend class.

Credit is given for independent study projects, correspondence courses, and a thesis or creative project.

Students may pursue the degree entirely in one of the five areas, or by following a curriculum that includes and integrates all five areas. Each course is accompanied by a study guide. Grading is based on written assignments. Professors guide students through courses by means of mail, telephone, and cassettes. At least 30 semester hours are required for the degree. Eighty percent must be earned after enrolling. A full-time student can finish in one academic year.

This is an unusual opportunity to earn an accredited Master's degree nonresidentially from a major university. My wife completed her M.A. in philosophy here in 1985, at a time when we were living in a remote rural location, and she could not have earned such a degree in any other way.

Central Michigan University

Accredited off-campus Bachelor's and Master's in various fields. If you can organize a large enough local group anywhere, the university will come to you.

Extended Degree Program, Rowe Hall 131
Mt. Pleasant, MI 48859

Telephone: (517) 774-3868
Fax: (517) 774-3537

Toll-free phone: (800) 950-1144
Year Established: 1892

Degree levels: Bachelor's, Master's
Key person: Robert Trullinger
Accreditation: Accredited
Ownership status: Nonprofit, state
Residency: Nonresident
Cost index: $$

Fields of study or special interest:
Bachelor of Science in community development, administration; Master of Science in administration; Master of Arts in community leadership or education

Other information:
Students can earn a general administration degree or specialize in health services administration or public administration. Intensive classes are given at many locations around the U.S. All programs are operated under the sponsorship of companies, military bases, or professional organizations. In most cases, anyone may enroll, whether or not they have an association with the sponsor.

The University maintains extended degree program offices in four states (Michigan, Virginia, Hawaii, and Missouri) and program centers in dozens more, plus two in Alberta, Canada.

At the Bachelor's level, one semester of credit (15 units) can also be earned through correspondence study.

Degree programs are structured to meet the needs of groups in each area, so not all courses are available at all centers. The University will consider offering a Master's program at any location where enough students can be enrolled. For the Master's, 21 semester hours (of the 36 required) must be completed through CMU. Up to 10 units can come from prior learning assessment.

Charter Oak State College

Accredited Associate's and Bachelor's degrees through home study at a low cost.

270 Farmington Avenue
Farmington, CT 06032

Telephone: (203) 677-0076
Fax: (203) 677-5147

Toll-free phone: (800) 842-2220 (CT only)
Year established: 1973

Degree levels: Bachelor's
Key person: Helen Giliberto
Accreditation: Accredited
Ownership status: Nonprofit, state
Residency: Nonresident
Cost index: $$

Fields of study or special interest:
Many fields of study

Other information:
The college is operated by the Connecticut Board for State Academic Awards, and offers the Bachelor of Arts, and Bachelor of Science degrees. The student is responsible for amassing 120 semester units (or 60 for the Associate's), which may come from courses taken elsewhere, equivalency examinations, military study, correspondence courses, or portfolio reviews. As soon as the 120 units are earned, with at least half in the arts and sciences, and 36 in a single subject or major area, the degree is awarded. Degrees are awarded in a large number of fields of study, including business, mathematics, science and technology, behavioral sciences, human services, humanities, and social sciences. Original name: Connecticut Board for State Academic Achievement Awards; later, Charter Oak College.

City University

Accredited nonresident Associate's, Bachelor's, and Master's through home study, with the option of using a home computer to communicate with the school.

16661 Northup Way
Bellevue, WA 98008

Telephone: (206) 643-2000   **Toll-free phone:** (800) 426-5596
Fax: (206) 637-9689   **Year established:** 1973

Degree levels: Bachelor's, Master's
Key person: Robert Van Woert, Ed.D.
Accreditation: Accredited
Ownership status: Nonprofit, independent
Residency: Nonresident
Cost index: $$$

Fields of study or special interest:

Business administration and management (many specialized areas), health care administration, computer science, nursing, accounting, finance, education, and aviation management. Other fields by special arrangement.

Other information:

Distance learning degrees in business, health care administration, accounting, and finance are offered entirely by home computer (using e-mail), or by more traditional means. City University offers programs in 26 Washington cities and in Portland, Oregon; Santa Clara, California; several British Columbia locations; Zurich, Switzerland; and Frankfurt, Germany, leading to a Bachelor's in Business Administration or Health Care Administration, the M.B.A., M.P.A. (public administration), and A B.S.N. (nursing) program is offered through evening study, and programs in computer science by evening or weekend study.

Degrees in business and public administration are also offered via distance learning anywhere in the world. PLE (prior learning experience program) allows students to get credit for life experience. Following a course in portfolio preparation, the portfolio is evaluated by a review committee to determine how many credits the student will be given (maximum 45). An instructor is assigned to each distance learner for each course. The student gets a course outline, textbook, assignments, tests, etc. Students may communicate with their instructors by mail or with computer modems. Courses must be finished in ten weeks. Research papers are required for most courses. Midterm and final exams are given locally by proctors. Students with special fields of interest may request a "panel for directed study" consisting of at least one senior faculty member and an expert in the field who will work out with the student an independent study course.

Colorado State University

Accredited Master's degrees in scientific fields, business, and computer science are offered by videotape to participating sites at other universities, businesses, etc.

SURGE Program, Division of Continuing Education
Spruce Hall
Fort Collins, CO 80523

Telephone: (303) 491-5288
Fax: (303) 491-7885

Toll-free phone: (800) 525-4950
Year established: 1870

Degree levels: Master's
Key person: Debbie Sheaman
Accreditation: Accredited
Ownership status: Nonprofit, state
Residency: Nonresident
Cost index: $$

Fields of study or special interest:
Engineering (agricultural, chemical, civil, electrical, mechanical), business administration, computer science, statistics

Other information:
The Colorado SURGE program is an innovative method of delivering graduate education to working professionals who cannot attend regular on-campus classes. Established in 1967, it was the first video-based graduate education program of its kind in America. An average of 80 courses are taught each semester via SURGE, from 17 departments in the Colleges of Agricultural Sciences, Applied Human Sciences, Business, Engineering, Natural Sciences, and Veterinary Medicine. Regular Colorado State graduate course are videotaped and sent, with other materials, to participating site coordinators. Site coordinators make these tapes and materials available to students, provide information about the program, supply registration forms, and proctor exams. Tapes are not sent to individual students. See also: Mind Extension University.

Columbia Pacific University

Unaccredited Bachelor's, Master's, Doctorates, and law degrees from one of the largest and oldest nontraditional schools.

1415 3rd St.
San Rafael, CA 94901

Telephone: (415) 459-1650
Fax: (415) 459-5856

Toll-free phone: (800) 552-5522 in CA,
(800) 227-0119 outside CA
Year established: 1978

Degree levels: Bachelor's, Master's, Doctorate, Law
Key person: Richard L. Crews, M.D.
Accreditation: Unaccredited
Ownership status: Proprietary
Residency: Nonresident
Cost index: $$$

Fields of study or special interest:
Many fields

Other information:
Nonresident degrees in many fields through schools of Arts and Sciences, Administration and Management, and Health and Human Services. Degrees are based on credit for prior learning, completion of a core curriculum normally requiring 12 to 18 months (covering research methods, creative thinking, learning techniques, etc.), and a major project or dissertation.

Columbia Pacific claims to be the largest nontraditional school of its kind, with more than 5,000 students enrolled. Students complete CPU's "core curriculum" which consists of four "projects" of directed reading, workbook exercises, essays, self-assessment, and independent study. The structure of the curriculum is same for all, but students help shape their studies based on what they are particularly interested in studying. Each student completes a major project, thesis, or dissertation. There is a minimum enrollment time of nine months. A quarterly surcharge is added for persons who do not finish within one year. The law degree, in international law, is for people who wish to learn more law and have a law degree, but it does not qualify one to take the California bar exam.

Columbia Pacific operates from its own office building in San Rafael, near San Francisco, and from a "retreat center" in Petaluma, California. I served as a consultant to Columbia Pacific in its early years. I was paid partly in stock, which I disposed of when I became disinvolved in 1984, and I have had no connection since then.

Columbia Union College

Accredited Associate's and Bachelor's in many fields, entirely through correspondence study.

7600 Flower Avenue
Takoma Park, MD 20912

Telephone: (301) 270-9200
Fax: (301) 270-1618

Toll-free phone: ——
Year established: 1904

Degree levels: Associate's, Bachelor's
Key person: Charlotte Conway
Accreditation: Accredited
Ownership status: Nonprofit, church
Residency: Nonresident
Cost index: $$

Fields of study or special interest:

Associate's in general studies; Bachelor's in business administration, general studies, health care administration, respiratory therapy, religion

Other information:

In most programs, all work is done by correspondence courses. The student is sent a syllabus, textbooks, and assignments. All courses require proctored exams, which may be taken anywhere. Contact is maintained between student and instructor of each course through mail, phone, and progress evaluations. A short residency is required for the degree in health care administration (one two-week session) and respiratory therapy (two two-week sessions).

Credit is given for experiential learning when demonstrated through competency examinations. Maximum credit for this is 24 semester hours. Credit is also given for standard equivalency examinations or work experience after the student has earned at least 24 semester hours in the program. At least 30 units must be earned after enrolling at CU (representing between 8 and 12 courses.) All students must write a major paper, related to literature, science, religion, or arts or pass a comprehensive examination to qualify for graduation.

The school is operated by the Seventh-Day Adventist Church, but nonchurch members are welcome. Students may live anywhere in the world, but all work must be done in English.

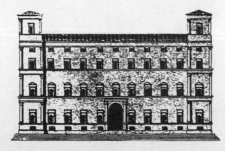

Cook's Institute of Electronics Engineering

Bachelor and Master of Science in Electronics Engineering and Master's in computer science entirely by home study.

Highway 18, P.O. Box 20345
Jackson, MS 39029

Telephone: (601) 371-1351   Toll-free phone: ——
Fax: ——   Year established: 1945

Degree levels: Bachelor's, Master's
Key person: Wallace L. Cook
Accreditation: Unaccredited
Ownership status: Proprietary
Residency: Nonresident
Cost index: $$$$

Fields of study or special interest:
Electronics engineering, computer science

Other information:
Bachelor and Master of Science in Electronics Engineering, entirely through correspondence study, involving completion of 36 courses. A thesis is required for the Master's. Advanced placement (and reduced tuition) is available for experienced electronic technicians with satisfactory prior schooling. At least 15 of the 36 courses must be completed after enrolling.

The school literature explains in great detail why they are not accredited by a recognized agency (no home study engineering program is), and makes clear the distinction between their B.S.E.E. and the correspondence B.S. in engineering technology offered by their chief competitor, Grantham.

Wallace Cook, the owner, established this school more than 45 years ago. Accreditation is from the unrecognized but legitimate National Association for Private Nontraditional Schools and Colleges.

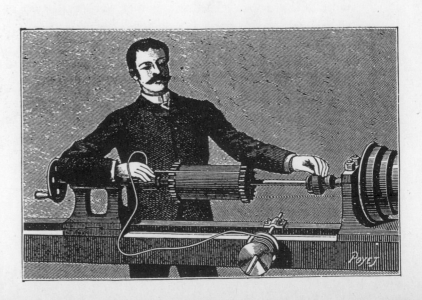

Eastern Illinois University

Accredited Bachelor of Arts can be earned entirely through independent study, equivalency exams, and credit for life experience learning.

Charleston, IL 61920

Telephone: (217) 581-5618
Fax: (217) 581-2722

Toll-free phone: ——
Year established: 1895

Degree levels: Bachelor's
Key person: Dr. Kaye Woodward
Accreditation: Accredited
Ownership status: Nonprofit, state
Residency: Nonresident
Cost index: $$

Fields of study or special interest:
Many fields

Other information:
Bachelor of Arts, with a minimum of 15 units to be earned on campus. Eastern Illinois is one of five members of the Board of Governors Bachelor of Arts program, a nontraditional program designed to allow working adults the chance to complete most of their requirements off-campus, through independent study, equivalency examinations, and credit for life experience.

A major is not required. Skills and knowledge acquired by nonacademic means can be evaluated for academic credit.

Eckerd College

Accredited Bachelor's degrees in liberal arts fields entirely through home study.

Program for Experienced Learners, P.O. Box 12560
St. Petersburg, FL 33733

Telephone: (813) 864-8226
Fax: (813) 866-2304

Toll-free phone: ——
Year established: 1959

Degree levels: Bachelor's
Key person: Dana E. Cozad
Accreditation: Accredited
Ownership status: Nonprofit, independent
Residency: Nonresident
Cost index: $$

Fields of study or special interest:
Many fields

Other information:
No physical residency is required, but students must complete at least nine courses through Eckerd College. Two correspondents report that Eckerd encouraged them to enroll in the evening program instead, saying that "most external students end up there anyway." Home study courses are prepared by faculty members. They require no classroom participation or campus residence. Students may enroll either in directed or independent study. Directed study means basic correspondence courses. Independent study is initiated by the student to meet special interests. The content and format of each course is determined by the supervising faculty member, and approved by the director of PEL.

Credit can be earned by examination. Credit for experiential learning is earned by taking a required course in how to document this learning. One learns how to prepare a portfolio which details what one has done. The portfolio is assessed by Eckerd faculty who determine the amount of credit to be awarded. The same course involves working out a degree plan covering the conditions that need to be met to earn the degree desired. Degree plans may also allow students to use current career experience as part of their program.

Interdisciplinary programs are also a possibility: a program tailored to individual student needs and wishes by the faculty . This may involve taking courses in various disciplines. Eckerd was originally called Florida Presbyterian College.

Electronic University Network

Accredited undergraduate and graduate study at various schools using a computer and modem to communicate with instructors.

1977 Colestin Road
Hornbrook, CA 96044

Telephone: (503) 482-5871   **Toll-free phone:** 800-22LEARN
Fax: (503) 482-7544   **Year established:** 1983

Degree levels: Associate;s, Bachelor's, Master's, Doctorate
Key person: Dr. Steve Eskow, President
Accreditation: Accredited
Ownership status: Proprietary
Residency: Nonresident
Cost index: $$$

Fields of study or special interest:
Business, liberal arts, psychology, integral studies

Other information:
The Electronic University Network links students anywhere in the world with accredited colleges and universities in the U.S. and Britain. Students sign on to the Electronic University Campus to exchange electronic mail with instructors and other students, participate in conferences, visit the Library, and join activities in the Student Union. The campus is accessed with IBM, Macintosh, or Apple II computers and software provided by America Online, the international computer network on which the campus is located.

Students earn external degrees from accredited institutions affiliated with the EUN. These currently include California Institute of Integral Studies (Ph.D.); Rogers State College (Associate's); Thomas A. Edison State College and Regents College of the University of New York (Associate's, Bachelor's); and Heriot-Watt University (M.B.A.). Enrollment is open entry/open exit. Students may begin at any time and proceed at their own pace. It is not necessary to be a degree candidate in order to take courses; many are open to all. Academic counseling is available online for those who want to earn a degree. Course fees include tuition, instruction, telecommunications costs, the printed course teleguide, and technical support. Textbooks and exam fees are extra.

A free EUN catalog on a diskette (no modem required) is available, as is free AOL software for those who have a modem. Printed catalogs cost $10.

Elizabethtown College

Accredited Bachelor's degrees in many fields, with a total of four days on campus, for people who live within 400 miles of the campus.

Elizabethtown, PA 17022

Telephone: (717) 367-1151
Fax: ——

Toll-free phone: (800) 877-2694
Year established: 1899

Degree levels: Bachelor's
Key person: Barbara R. Maroney
Accreditation: Accredited
Ownership status: Nonprofit, church
Residency: Short residency
Cost index: $$$

Fields of study or special interest:
Professional and liberal studies

Other information:
Bachelor of Professional Studies and Bachelor of Liberal Studies (religious studies), offered through the EXCEL program. Majors offered in the B.P.S. degree program are: accounting, business administration, communications, criminal justice, early childhood education (non-teaching certification), human services, medical technology, and public administration.

Applicants must have a minimum of seven years of work experience related to the major field of study and at least 50 semester hours of college study, grade C or better, at regionally accredited institutions and reside within 400 miles of the College. Credit awarded for CLEP/DANTE exams, certain structured noncredit learning, and (up to 32 semester hours) for experiential learning in the major field of study.

Embry-Riddle Aeronautical University

Accredited nonresident degrees in aviation and business subjects, entirely through home study.

Department of Independent Studies
Daytona Beach, FL 32119

Telephone: (904) 226-6397
Fax: (904) 239-6927

Toll-free phone: ——
Year established: 1926

Degree levels: Bachelor's
Key person: Thomas W. Pettit
Accreditation: Accredited
Ownership status: Nonprofit, independent
Residency: Nonresident
Cost index: $$$

Fields of study or special interest:
Aeronautics

Other information:
Bachelor of Science in professional aeronautics with no traditional classroom attendance. Applicants must have certified or military training and professional experience in any of the following: air traffic control, airways facilities, aviation weather, electronic operations, flight operations administration, navigation systems, certified flight instructor or pilot (airline command, air carrier, military, corporate, regional airline).

Up to 36 semester hours may be awarded for professional training and experience.

The Bachelor of Science in aviation business administration is also offered to people with no aviation experience.

Credit is given for CLEP and other exams and work at accredited schools. Tuition of $135 per semester hour includes guides and audiotapes. There is a rental fee of $20 for videotapes. Textbook prices vary.

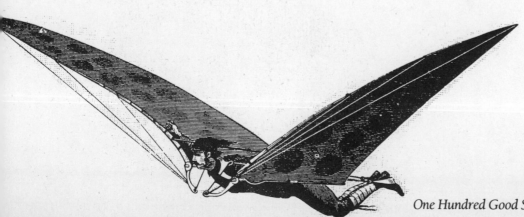

Empire State College

Accredited Associates, Bachelor's, and Master's in many fields. Master's requires eight days on campus; the others degrees are nonresidential.

2 Union Avenue
Saratoga Springs, NY 12866

Telephone: (518) 587-2100   Toll-free phone: (800) 468-4390 (NY only)
Fax: ——   Year established: 1971

Degree levels: Bachelor's, Master's
Key person: Theodore DiPadova
Accreditation: Accredited
Ownership status: Nonprofit, state
Residency: Nonresident
Cost index: $$

Fields of study or special interest:
Liberal arts, business and policy, human services

Other information:
A part of the State University of New York, Empire State College provides programs in 40 locations across New York state. The primary mode of study is independent study guided by faculty mentors. Together, students and mentors develop a degree program within the college's 11 broad areas of undergraduate study. Credit is given for college-level learning gained from work and other life experience.

The Bachelor's degrees can be completed entirely by independent, faculty-guided study; classroom attendance generally not required. The Master of Arts requires four days on campus at the beginning and end of each semester, and is offered in business and policy studies, labor and policy studies, and culture and policy studies. They combine independent study with three three-or-four day weekends on campus each year.

In addition, the Center for Distance Learning offers structured courses and degree programs in business administration, human services, and interdisciplinary studies for students seeking more structured learning but without classroom attendance or travel; faculty guidance is by mail and telephone.

Fernuniversität

Accredited Master's and Doctorates from Germany's distance teaching university in many fields entirely through home study plus examinations taken in Germany. All work is done in German.

Feithstrasse 152
D-5800 Hagen, Germany

Telephone: (23-31) 804-2408
Fax: (23-31) 804-2763

Toll-free phone: ——
Year established: 1974

Degree levels: Master's, Doctorate
Key person: Information Division
Accreditation: Accredited
Ownership status: Nonprofit, state
Residency: Nonresident
Cost index: $

Fields of study or special interest:
Many fields

Other information:
Germany's Distance Teaching University offers the Master's, Doctorate, and Diploma-Degree through completion of correspondence study units, plus examinations (which must be taken in Germany). Instruction is through a combination of written materials and audiocassettes. All courses are self-paced.

Courses are offered in the fields of mathematics, electrical engineering, computer science, economics, law, educational science, social science and the arts. The university operates about 63 study centers in Germany, Austria, Switzerland, and Hungary for the assistance and guidance of students.

All instruction is in German, although a nice color brochure is available in English. More than 1,450 of Fernuniversität's over 50,000 students live outside of Germany.

Ferris State University

Accredited Bachelor's in industrial or environmental health by home study plus a three-week summer session on campus.

Gerholz Institute for Lifelong Learning
Big Rapids, MI 49307

Telephone: (616) 592-2340
Fax: (616) 592-2990

Toll-free phone: (800) 562-9130 (MI only)
Year established: 1884

Degree levels: Bachelor's
Key person: Jeffrey Cross
Accreditation: Accredited
Ownership status: Nonprofit, state
Residency: Short residency
Cost index: $$

Fields of study or special interest:
Environmental health

Other information:
The Bachelor of Science in industrial and environmental health management is offered through the College of Allied Health Science as an external degree program for qualified students anywhere in the United States. (Three years of work experience in the field of environmental health is required for admission to the program.)

All of the requirements for the degree can be met through assessment of prior learning experience and a combination of equivalency examinations, independent study, faculty-directed study, home study courses, and special projects. All students must attend a three-week summer session on campus. Prior learning assessment can take as long as a year, and is done for a flat fee of around $250.

Off-campus programs in health systems management, nursing, business administration, computer information systems, accountancy, maritime management, and vocational/occupational education (manufacturing, engineering technology, automotive management, construction management) are available at selected sites in Michigan.

Fielding Institute

Accredited Master's and Doctorates in human and organization development, psychology and related areas, with a minimum of five days on campus.

2122 Santa Barbara Street
Santa Barbara, CA 93105

Telephone: (805) 687-1099
Fax: (805) 687-4590

Toll-free phone: ——
Year established: 1974

Degree levels: Master's, Doctorate
Key person: Sylvia Williams
Accreditation: Accredited
Ownership status: Nonprofit, independent
Residency: Short residency
Cost index: $$$$

Fields of study or special interest:
Psychology, human and organizational development

Other information:
The Human and Organizational Development Program offers an Ed.D., a Ph.D. in human and organizational systems or human development, a D.H.S. (Doctor of Human Services), and a Master's degree. The Psychology program offers a Ph.D. in clinical psychology. The program is designed for midcareer professionals. It typically takes three to six years to complete a doctoral degree, but only five days are required on campus. Qualified applicants attend an Admissions Contract Workshop where a learning contract is developed. Workshops are held three times a year.

The psychology program requires attendance at local student meetings. Students meet regularly with Fielding faculty (cluster facilitators) for knowledge assessment, dissertation reviews, seminars, and peer contact and support. There are dozens of clusters located throughout the U.S. Work typically consists of guided independent study, research papers, exams, lectures, and professional reports. The psychology degrees emphasize clinical or counseling and include a practicum and internship, research training, a dissertation, and an oral review. Although there are no rigid requirements about residency, there are times when a psychology student should be available to come to campus.

Fielding does not accept transfer credit or give credit for prior experiential learning. All students and faculty must have access to a computer with communication capability, used for electronic mail, bulletin board service, and academic seminars.

Goddard College

Accredited Bachelor's and Master's in feminist studies, performing arts, and other fields, requiring several nine-day sessions on campus.

Plainfield, VT 05667

Telephone: (802) 454-8311
Fax: (802) 454-8017

Toll-free phone: (800) 468-4888
Year established: 1938

Degree levels: Bachelor's, Master's
Key person: Peter Burns
Accreditation: Accredited
Ownership status: Nonprofit, independent
Residency: Nonresident
Cost index: $$$

Fields of study or special interest:

Many fields, including business, history, visual and performing arts, multicultural studies, communications, literature, teacher education, and feminist studies

Other information:

Goddard has been a pioneer in nontraditional, progressive education for more than 55 years. They offer nontraditional options for studies in business and organizational leadership, education, psychology and counseling, natural and physical sciences, feminist studies, the visual and performing arts, literature and writing, and social and cultural studies (history, philosophy, religious studies). The first nine days of each semester are spent in residency, where the work of the coming semester is planned. Students may choose to be "off-campus students," in which case the majority of work is done off-campus while maintaining contact by mail every three weeks. Minimum enrollment is two semesters for the Bachelor's, three for the Master's. Credit is available for prior learning, but life experience credit is given only at the Bachelor's level.

Learning comes through doing (reading, writing, experimenting, creating, observing, etc.), and reflecting on doing (talking, journals, etc.). Each student must write a letter-report to his or her faculty advisor every three weeks. At the next nine-day meeting the student presents work done and is evaluated by self, advisor, and fellow students.

Students are expected to devote a minimum of 26 hours per week to study.

Goddard has worked with clusters of students at various locations around the U.S. and in Europe, where residential requirements could be met.

Graceland College

Accredited Bachelor of Science in Nursing for working registered nurses, through clinical work in one's own community plus two weeks a year on campus.

Outreach Program
Division of Nursing
Lamoni, IA 50140

Telephone: (515) 784-5000
Fax: (515) 784-5480

Toll-free phone: (800) 537-6276
Year established: 1895

Degree levels: Bachelor's
Key person: Lewis Smith Jr.
Accreditation: Accredited
Ownership status: Nonprofit, church
Residency: Short residency
Cost index: $$$

Fields of study or special interest:
Nursing, liberal studies

Other information:
The program is designed for working RN's.

Home study-texts, learning guides (developed by Graceland faculty), and videotapes are used. Courses include projects, tests, and final proctored exam. There is a toll-free number so students can talk to instructors.

Up to 64 hours of advanced placement toward the Bachelor of Arts in liberal studies can come through evaluation of nursing education and experience.

The Bachelor of Science in Nursing program has clinical components. A student can come to campus or find a college-approved preceptor to monitor their progress in their own community.

Residency sessions occur twice a year for two weeks and are required.

Grantham College of Engineering

Accredited Bachelor's degree in engineering technology entirely by home study.

34641 Grantham College Road
P.O. Box 5700
Slidell, LA 70469

Telephone: (504) 649-4191
Fax: (504) 649-4183

Toll-free phone: (800) 955-2527
Year established: 1951

Degree levels: Bachelor's
Key person: Mark P. Dean
Accreditation: Accredited
Ownership status: Proprietary
Residency: Nonresident
Cost index: $$

Fields of study or special interest:
Engineering technology

Other information:
Nonresident Bachelor's degrees in engineering technology, with an emphasis in either computers or electronics. Grantham's programs are designed for people who already have practical experience in the field and laboratory. Students are given up to two years to complete the self-paced home-study courses, but a highly motivated person could complete all 402 lessons and 8 exams in one year. All applicants must have already completed 21 unit-hours elsewhere (in English, history, etc.) and must have access to a personal computer.

Grantham awards up to 18 units of credit for work experience and lab proficiency. Work is done through correspondence courses and independent home study. Mid-phase and end of phase exams are given locally by proctors approved by the school.

The Associate's degree is awarded "along the way" to the Bachelor's, after phase three.

Grantham's main rival, Cook's Institute, makes a big point of the fact that Cook's degree is in electronics engineering, while Grantham's is in engineering technology.

In 1990, Grantham moved from California to Louisiana.

Greenwich University

Unaccredited nonresident Bachelor's, Master's, Doctorates, and law degrees from one of the oldest schools of its kind in the U.S.

100 Kamehameha Avenue
Hilo, HI 96720

Telephone: (808) 935-9934
Fax: (808) 969-7469

Toll-free phone: (800) FOR-HILO
Year established: 1972

Degree levels: Bachelor's, Master's, Doctorate, Law
Key person: Stuart Johnson, Ed.D.
Accreditation: Unaccredited
Ownership status: Proprietary
Residency: Nonresident
Cost index: $$

Fields of study or special interest:

Degrees can be earned in almost any field of study. There is a non-bar-qualifying law degree program (J.D.) for medical doctors.

Other information:

Greenwich evolved from the International Institute for Advanced Studies, the oldest nontraditional graduate school in the U.S. Each student's learning (however it occurred) is matched against standards for what a degree-holder should know. Greenwich then helps the student fill in any "gaps" in that learning, through guided independent study using a learning contract developed by student and faculty mentors. A major paper, thesis, or dissertation is required; it may be based on work done before enrolling.

The adjunct faculty of 150 include many prominent scholars and authors. The Greenwich University School of Theology is based in England; there is an affiliation with an accredited school of art and design in New Zealand, with other schools in Europe and Asia, and there is an office in Australia. The main administrative center is the oceanfront Greenwich University Building in Hilo, Hawaii's second largest city.

In 1993, Greenwich was moving through the accreditation process with the Pacific Association of Schools and Colleges, an unrecognized but reputable accreditor that was, itself, moving through the recognition process with the U.S. Department of Education.

For five years, I was the full-time president of Greenwich (and its predecessor, the International Institute), and of course I wouldn't have done it if I didn't think it was a good school and program. (I am now president emeritus.)

Henley, the Management College

Accredited British M.B.A. through correspondence study plus examinations taken in England, Asia, or Australia.

Greenlands
Henley-on-Thames, Oxon. RG9 3AU England

Telephone: (44-491) 571-454   Toll-free phone: ——
Fax: (44-491) 571-635   Year established: 1946

Degree levels: Master's
Key person: Jill Ford, Admissions Manager, Graduate Studies
Accreditation: Accredited
Ownership status: Nonprofit, independent
Residency: Short residency
Cost index: $$$

Fields of study or special interest:
Business administration

Other information:
Henley offers its nonresident M.B.A. in association with Brunel University, which awards the degree. Courses include texts, case studies, and audio- and videocassettes. Exams are held either at Henley, at one of the Henley Network Centers worldwide, at a local educational establishment or a British Council Office.

Students write a dissertation (up to 60 pages), ideally dealing with a real problem for their own organization. There is tutorial support via computer. The computer may also be used to initiate conferences with fellow users and participate in conferences which are set up by experts in a particular field.

Workshops are offered for meeting tutors and fellow students prior to beginning the program and prior to exams. Workshops are considered to be desirable but not compulsory. They are given at Henley and other institutions affiliated with Henley Network Centers throughout the world (Australia, Cyprus, Denmark, Finland, Hong Kong, Malaysia, the Netherlands, Singapore, and three more in England). The degree may be completed in a "standard" three and a half year program, or an accelerated two year program. Applicants must have a Bachelor's degree and at least two years organizational experience. A list of participants within the same area is available to all students. They are encouraged to form study and support groups.

Heriot-Watt University

Accredited international M.B.A. from an old Scottish university entirely through home study; no Bachelor's degree required, no entrance exams.

North American Agency
1780 Shattuck Avenue
Berkeley, CA 94709

Telephone: (510) 204-9995   Toll-free phone: (800) MBA-0707
Fax: (510) 841-8771   Year established: 1821

Degree levels: Master's
Key person: Dr. John Bear, North American Agency
Accreditation: Accredited
Ownership status: Nonprofit, state
Residency: Nonresident
Cost index: $$$

Fields of study or special interest:
Business administration

Other information:
The Distance Learning M.B.A. was introduced in 1990, and has grown rapidly to become one of the largest M.B.A.s in the world. *The Economist* magazine calls it "one of the world's best MBA programmes," along with Harvard, Wharton, Stanford, Cambridge, etc. The M.B.A. curriculum consists of nine courses (marketing, economics, finance, strategic planning, etc.). Each comes self-contained in a box for $685 which includes course fees, text materials, and university registration. Each course requires a three-hour examination which may be taken almost anywhere in the world. Optional computer software is available at extra cost for many courses. This is a rigorous program for serious students who wish to be challenged intellectually.

I have opened a Heriot-Watt agency to serve students in North America. Most company employee reimbursement plans will pay the tuition. Approvals have come from AT&T, Dupont, IBM, American Express, Federal Express, United Parcel, Lockheed, Digital, Hewlett-Packard, and many other major corporations as well as by the U.S. government for employees in various governmental departments.

Heriot-Watt's admission policy is "open access" which means that no Bachelor's degree is required, and there are no entrance exams. The university believes that anyone who can pass their courses deserves their degree. Address in Scotland: Heriot-Watt University, Edinburgh EH14 4AS. The telephone is (44-31) 451-3090, and the fax is (44-31) 451-3002.

Indiana University

Accredited Bachelor of General Studies, with no major or with a major in labor studies, entirely by correspondence study.

External Degree Program, Division of Extended Studies
Indiana University, Owen Hall 101
Bloomington, IN 47405

Telephone: (812) 855-3692
Fax: (812) 855-0431

Toll-free phone: (800) 334-1011 outside IN
(800) 342-5410 in IN
Year established: 1975

Degree levels: Bachelor's
Key person: Louis R. Holtzclaw
Accreditation: Accredited
Ownership status: Nonprofit, state
Residency: Nonresident
Cost index: $$

Fields of study or special interest:
General studies

Other information:
The Bachelor of General Studies is available entirely through nonresidential study. The degree can be done without a major. One hundred twenty semester units are required, of which at least 30 must be earned from Indiana University. All 30 can be via independent study by correspondence. One quarter of the units must be upper division (junior or senior) level. The university also has evening courses, a Weekend College, and a course to assist in developing a life experience portfolio.

A comparable degree can be done through Indiana University Southeast, School for Continuing Studies, 4201 Grant Line Road, New Albany, IN 47150.

Indiana University of Pennsylvania

Accredited Ph.D. in English and American literature or in rhetoric and linguistics with two summer sessions on campus plus independent study in between.

Indiana, PA 15705

Telephone: (412) 357-2222
Fax: (412) 357-6213

Toll-free phone: ——
Year established: 1875

Degree levels: Doctorate
Key person: Dr. Evelyn S. Mutchnick
Accreditation: Accredited
Ownership status: Nonprofit, state
Residency: Short residency
Cost index: $$

Fields of study or special interest:
English and American Literature

Other information:
Indiana University of Pennsylvania offers two Ph.D.s in English: one in English and American Literature and the second in rhetoric and linguistics. Basic coursework can be completed in two consecutive summers of full-time study, with independent study in between.

Programs are arranged to accommodate secondary, community, and four-year college teachers, allowing graduate students to pursue their studies without interrupting their careers. Students can choose from a number of areas related to the humanistic study of literature, including psychology, history, art, and music. Candidacy, comprehensive exams, and a dissertation are required. The language requirement can be met by coursework, exams, or proficiency in a computer language.

This is a rigorous program for serious students who wish to be challenged intellectually.

Institute for the Advanced Study of Human Sexuality

Unaccredited Master's and Doctorates in various aspects of human sexuality, largely through home and independent study.

1523 Franklin Street
San Francisco, CA 94109

Telephone: (415) 928-1133   Toll-free phone: ——
Fax: ——   Year established: 1976

Degree levels: Master's, Doctorate
Key person: Robert T. McIlvenna, M.Div., Ph.D.
Accreditation: Unaccredited
Ownership status: Proprietary
Residency: Short residency
Cost index: $$$

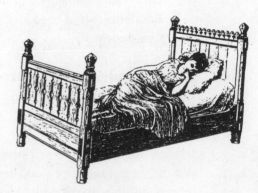

Fields of study or special interest:
Human sexuality, erotology, sex offender evaluation

Other information:
The Institute believes there is a "woeful lack of professionals who are academically prepared in the study of human sexuality." The Institute's intention is to rectify this lack by training professionals as sexologists. Degrees offered include Master of Human Sexuality, Doctor of Human Sexuality (for therapists), Doctor of Education (for educators), and Doctor of Philosophy (stressing new knowledge and scientific inquiry). They also offer certificates in: sexological instructor of AIDS/STD prevention, erotology, and sex offender evaluation. Each Doctorate has a different emphasis: one in scientific inquiry, one in academic skills, and one in therapy and counseling.

There are three trimesters per year. A short time must be spent on campus for attending courses and lectures, but most work can be done at home. Many lectures are available on videotape. A comprehensive exam and a basic research project are required. The Master's requires three trimesters of enrollment, and the Doctoral programs require five trimesters each.

Founders include prominent sexologists, such as Kinsey's coauthor, Wardell Pomeroy. The Institute is accredited by the unrecognized but legitimate National Association for Private Nontraditional Schools and Colleges.

International Correspondence Schools

Accredited Associate's in business by correspondence, and in technology with a one-week residency from America's pioneer correspondence school.

Center for Degree Studies
Scranton, PA 18515

Telephone: (717) 342-7701   Toll-free phone: ——
Fax: ——   Year established: 1890

Degree levels: Associate's
Key person: James S. Petorak, Director, Research and Testing
Accreditation: Accredited
Ownership status: Proprietary
Residency: Nonresident
Cost index: $$

Fields of study or special interest:
Associate in Specialized Business degree in business management or accounting; Associate in Specialized Technology degree in civil, electrical, and mechanical engineering and electronics technologies

Other information:
America's first significant correspondence school arose in Pennsylvania during the 1890s to provide education to coal miners. Now they provide it to untold thousands, through home study courses in business and technology.

Students are assigned work from courses produced by ICS. Instructors correct assignments, make criticisms, and can modify the program to meet the needs of each student.

Additional information is available through printed supplements to the courses, and a telecommunications network which links the student to the central office.

There are final exams at the end of each semester which may be taken locally, with a proctor selected by ICS.

The business degree can be completed entirely by correspondence; the technology degree requires a residency of about one week.

International School of Information Management

Unaccredited nonresident Master's in information management, which can be earned entirely by use of a home computer.

130 Cremona Drive
P. O. Box 1999
Santa Barbara, CA 93116

Telephone: (805) 685-1500
Fax: ——

Toll-free phone: (800) 441-4746
Year established: 1982

Degree levels: Master's
Key person: Eric H. Boem, Ph.D., President
Accreditation: Unaccredited
Ownership status: Proprietary
Residency: Nonresident
Cost index: $$$$

Fields of study or special interest:
Information resources management

Other information:
The instruction is delivered via a computer teleconferencing network. The program is available to students in U.S. and Canada now; the rest of the world comes later.

Students need to be "teleliterate," and have a computer and telephone modem. The Institute offers a teleliteracy course on a tutorial basis. For each course, the student receives a complete study guide, communications software, and study materials, such as textbooks and other written materials. Methods vary from instructor to instructor as to how competence is demonstrated, whether by projects, papers, written assignments, tests, etc.

Most coursework will be sent to the instructor by computer. Visual materials or materials not suitable for transmission via telecommunications may be sent by mail. Each course provides a public discussion area open to all course participants, who interact by computer conferencing. This area provides an open forum for discussions between students and faculty on topics relating to the course.

Iowa State University

Accredited Bachelor of Liberal Studies available entirely by home study.

College of Sciences and Humanities
204 Carver Hall
Ames, IA 50011

Telephone: (515) 294-5836
Fax: (515) 294-0565

Toll-free phone: (800) 262-3810
Year established: 1858

Degree levels: Bachelor's, Master's
Key person: Karsten Smedal
Accreditation: Accredited
Ownership status: Nonprofit, state
Residency: Short residency
Cost index: $$

Fields of study or special interest:
Many fields

Other information:
The university offers an external Bachelor of Liberal Studies, primarily for residents of Iowa who are able to attend one of the off-campus centers around the state or occasional courses on the Ames campus, although such attendance is not mandatory. Previous Iowa State students with sufficient credit may also be eligible for the program.

The program is designed specifically for those who have already earned 62 or more semester hours of college credit that may be applied to a liberal arts degree.

To complete a degree, students may earn credits through many study formats: television and tele-bridge courses, evening and weekend classes, on-campus classes, and correspondence classes. Students should check with an advisor to make sure any course they take will be acceptable to their degree program.

Of 124 units, 45 must come from a four-year college, 45 from one of Iowa Regents Universities, and 30 from Iowa State University. No traditional majors are available. Students choose to earn credits in three of five distribution areas (humanities, communications and arts, natural sciences and mathematical disciplines, social sciences, professional fields).

Judson College

Accredited nonresident Bachelor's degrees for women only in many fields, based on learning contracts.

Adult Degree Program
Marion, AL 36756

Telephone: (205) 683-6161
Fax: (205) 683-6161

Toll-free phone: ——
Year established: 1838

Degree levels: Bachelor's
Key person: Adult Degree Program
Accreditation: Accredited
Ownership status: Nonprofit, church
Residency: Nonresident
Cost index: $$$

Fields of study or special interest:

Art, biology, business administration, chemistry, computers, criminal justice, English, fashion merchandising, home economics, history, interior design, mathematics, psychology, religion, sociology

Other information:

This old Baptist women's college now allows men to take classes but not to earn degrees. At least one year of study (30 semester units) must be earned at Judson after enrolling. This can be done by taking traditional classes or through independent study based on a learning contract developed between the student and Judson faculty.

The college maintains an office in Huntsville, Alabama.

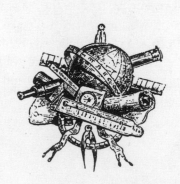

Kansas State University

Accredited nonresident Bachelor's in interdisciplinary studies.

Nontraditional Study Program, Umberger Hall
Division of Continuing Education
225 College Court
Manhattan, KS 66506

Telephone: (913) 532-5687
Fax: (913) 532-5637

Toll-free phone: (800) 432-8222 (KS),
(800) 622-2KSU elsewhere
Year established: 1863

Degree levels: Bachelor's
Key person: Cynthia Trent
Accreditation: Accredited
Ownership status: Nonprofit, state
Residency: Nonresident
Cost index: $$

Fields of study or special interest:
Interdisciplinary social science and agriculture, animal sciences and industry

Other information:
Kansas State University's Nontraditional Study program offers two Bachelor's degree completion programs: the Bachelor of Science in interdisciplinary social science, and the Bachelor of Science in agriculture, animal sciences and industry with an animal products option.

Applicants to the NTS program must already have earned at least 60 semester college credits toward either the B.S. in social science (a 120 credit-hour program) or the B.S. in agriculture (127 credit-hours total). Students may transfer up to 90 hours to KSU, and assessment of prior learning is available after one has been accepted into the program.

Students must earn at least 30 credits from KSU classes, which can be accomplished through television courses, cablecast across the United States on MEU, the education network. See page 106.

Kennedy-Western University

Unaccredited nonresident Bachelor's, Master's, Doctorate, and Law degrees.

1459 Tyrell Lane
Boise, ID 83706

Telephone: (208) 375-5402   Toll-free phone: (800) 635-2900
Fax: ——   Year established: 1984

Degree levels: Bachelor's, Master's, Doctorate, Law
Key person: Paul Saltman
Accreditation: Unaccredited
Ownership status: Proprietary
Residency: Nonresident
Cost index: $$

Fields of study or special interest:
Many fields, including business, health administration, criminal justice, education, and law

Other information:
A formal interview, in person or by telephone, is required before enrollment. Bachelor's applicants must have 60 semester units at college level or take a qualifying examination. All applicants must have five to seven years' experience in their field of study. Credit is given for experiential learning, as well as prior college work, and challenge exams.

New work is done through independent study. The student completes a study plan which sets forth goals, methods of meeting goals, time schedule, and criteria for evaluation of learning. The student's work will include such things as book critiques, case studies, and work-related research projects. All students must complete either a research project or term paper, or a thesis or dissertation. Students who feel they have a "sophisticated level of expertise in their field and have already published" may petition for a final exam instead.

Academic work may be done in English or sixteen other languages. Kennedy-Western was originally established in California.

Kensington University

Unaccredited nonresident Bachelor's, Master's, Doctorates, and Law degrees.

124 South Isabel Street
Glendale, CA 92106

Telephone: (818) 240-9166
Fax: (818) 240-1707

Toll-free phone: (800) 421-9115 (CA),
(800) 423-2495 (elsewhere)
Year established: 1976

Degree levels: Bachelor's, Master's, Doctorate, Law
Key person: James H. Lambert, Ph.D.
Accreditation: Unaccredited
Ownership status: Proprietary
Residency: Nonresident
Cost index: $$

Fields of study or special interest:
Business, engineering, social sciences, education, law

Other information:
Programs are designed for the mature adult student who is committed to self-directed study. All required coursework is accomplished by individual study, with guidance and instruction provided by faculty mentors. Most coursework consists of assigned texts/exams and projects. A study plan is developed for each individual student. Non-required seminars and programs are offered periodically, nationally and in Italy, Thailand, Japan, and England (where residential programs are available at the Bachelor's and Master's level through the facilities of City Commercial College in London).

Law students qualify to take the California bar exam, where they have had good success in recent years. Kensington's bar preparation program (called Inns of Court) requires four years. Entering students must already have 60 semester units of college work. Each student is assigned a faculty advisor, who is a practicing attorney, to assist the student in all aspects of study. The advisor is available by phone or personal conference. Non-bar programs, (called Inns of Chancery) are for those who "do not wish to actively engage in the practice of law, but nevertheless wish to gain a better understanding of legal principles and procedures."

Kensington's literature reports the findings of a government study on the acceptance of nontraditional degrees without making clear that this study was of accredited Bachelor's degrees only, and has no relevance to unaccredited or graduate degrees.

Lesley College

Accredited Bachelor's and Master's in science and education by independent study with two ten-day sessions on campus.

29 Everett Street
Cambridge, MA 02238

Telephone: (617) 868-9600
Fax: (617) 349-8717

Toll-free phone: (800) 999-1959
Year established: 1909

Degree levels: Bachelor's, Master's
Key person: Kimberly J. Kautz
Accreditation: Accredited
Ownership status: Nonprofit, independent
Residency: Short residency
Cost index: $$$$

Fields of study or special interest:
Many fields

Other information:
The Intensive Residency Option alternates ten days of on-campus work (during which plans are made for the next six months) with six months of independent study, leading to the Bachelor's degree.

There is a Bachelor of Science in cooperation with the National Audubon Society, involving a combination of coursework and expeditions. Audubon's Expedition Institute has a two-year program, or a field component: camping, hiking, canoeing, skiing, backpacking, and cycling all over America. Students gain practical knowledge of astronomy, anthropology, ecology, etc. The balance of the time is spent in classes at Lesley. The M.S. involves a year or a year and a half on Audubon expeditions and three or four courses at Lesley. Students may switch between Lesley and Audubon.

The M.A. and Master of Education are offered as an Independent Study Degree Program, allowing individualized curricula developed by graduate students and faculty advisory teams. Students typically meet four times on campus with their faculty during the course of the degree program. All other work is done through independent study, directed readings, tutorials, apprenticeships, etc. The cost is in excess of $10,000.

Loma Linda University

Accredited Master's degrees in health administration and health promotion through independent study and three-day intensive meetings with faculty at locations throughout the United States.

School of Public Health
Office of Extended Programs
Nichol Hall #1706
Loma Linda, CA 92350

Telephone: (714) 824-4595
Fax: (714) 824-4577

Toll-free phone: (800) 854-5661
Year established: 1905

Degree levels: Master's
Key person: Dr. Glen Blix
Accreditation: Accredited
Ownership status: Nonprofit, church
Residency: Nonresident
Cost index: $$$

Fields of study or special interest:
Public health (health promotion and health administration)

Other information:
The Extended Program at Loma Linda University's School of Public Health offers a practical way for mid-career health professionals to obtain a Master of Public Health (M.P.H.) degree while maintaining their present employment. The format includes a combination of independent study (pre- and post-lecture assignments) and extensive student/instructor contact.

The student is not required to spend time on campus at Loma Linda, rather instructors travel to various sites in the United States to meet with students in intensive three-day class sessions. One class per quarter is offered at each site. The program is geared to the needs of physicians, dentists, nurses, and other health professionals desiring to become qualified to organize health programs, to engage in health promotion activities, etc. The two majors available are health promotion and health administration.

Mary Baldwin College

Accredited Bachelor's degree in many fields, entirely by home study, except for one or two days on campus in Virginia.

Adult Degree Program
Staunton, VA 24401

Telephone: (703) 887-7003
Fax: (703) 886-5561

Toll-free phone: ——
Year established: 1842

Degree levels: Bachelor's
Key person: James P. McPherson
Accreditation: Accredited
Ownership status: Nonprofit, church
Residency: Short residency
Cost index: $$$$

Fields of study or special interest:
Many fields

Other information:
Mary Baldwin offers an accredited Bachelor of Arts program in which all of the work can be done independently, or at a distance. Students need to come to the campus only once for a day of orientation. Advanced standing is given for work done at other schools, equivalency examinations, and the assessment of prior learning. New work is done either by taking classes on campus, doing independent study under the guidance of Mary Baldwin faculty or local tutors, taking correspondence courses from other schools, or pursuing travel/study courses.

The degree program has regional offices in Richmond, Charlottesville, and Roanoke, Virginia, in addition to the main office in Staunton. The degree requires a minimum of nine months to complete.

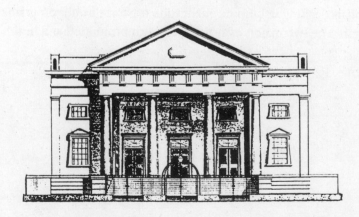

Marywood College

Accredited Bachelor's degrees in accounting or business administration by correspondence plus one or two two-week sessions on campus.

2300 Adams Avenue
Scranton, PA 18509

Telephone: (717) 348-6235
Fax: (717) 348-1817

Toll-free phone: (800) 836-6940
Year established: 1915

Degree levels: Bachelor's
Key person: Patrick J. Manley
Accreditation: Accredited
Ownership status: Nonprofit, church
Residency: Short residency
Cost index: $$

Fields of study or special interest:
Business administration, accounting

Other information:
The Bachelor of Science degree in accounting or business administration is earned through a combination of distance-learning (114 credits) and two two-week residencies (12 credits) held on the campus: one midway through the program, and one near the end. A minimum of 60 of the required 126 credits must be earned after enrolling at Marywood. Transfer credit is available through the evaluation of prior learning. The tuition fee per credit is $175, excluding the cost of study materials. A deferred tuition payment plan is available as well as financial aid for those who qualify. Program technology includes audio- and videotapes as well as electronic mail.

Students must be at least 18 years old and live more than 50 miles from Marywood. Credit is given for experiential learning (nearly half the required credit can come from this as well as equivalency exams). Courses are conducted by guided independent study. The student is sent "instruction units" consisting of texts, study guide, and assignments. Communication with teachers is by mail and phone. Courses require proctored exams. Credit can also be earned by completing independent study projects.

A student who has substantial transfer credit will have to spend only one two-week session on campus. Other students must spend two two-week periods on campus, one midway through the program, and one at the end.

nd Extension University

DAWN SCHNEIDER
AFFILIATE RELATIONS

Credits from various schools and an accredited M.B.A. from Colorado State University can be earned entirely through courses offered by cable television.

9697 East Mineral Avenue
P.O. Box 3309
Englewood, CO 80155

Telephone: —
Fax: —

Toll-free phone: (800) 777-MIND
Year established: —

Degree levels: Bachelor's, Master's
Key person: ME/U Education Center
Accreditation: Accredited
Ownership status: Independent
Residency: Nonresident
Cost index: $$$$

Fields of study or special interest:
Many fields

Other information:

Mind Extension University televises courses 24 hours a day over the university's own cable channel, nationwide. Some courses are also available by satellite or by purchasing videotapes. The individual courses are produced by different universities. Class materials and coursework are sent by mail. MEU provides a toll-free number to facilitate phone communication between student and instructor. All students logistics, except for academic evaluation and transcript documentation, occur between the student and the MEU Education Center. Exams given by a local proctor.

A student enrolls in MEU and receives credit from one of the MEU affiliated schools. At this time, three complete degree programs are offered: a Bachelor's in management through the University of Maryland, an M.B.A. from Colorado State University, and an M.A. in education and human development with a major in educational technology leadership, from George Washington University. The M.B.A. requires 63 semester units, although some may be waived if the equivalent work has been done elsewhere.

For people who do not have access to the MEU channel, it may be possible to buy or rent M.B.A. videotapes directly from Colorado State University. (I have spent a fair amount of time watching MEU on my local cable channel. The courses are prepared by each individual instructor and, just like on-campus education, range from lively and engaging to dry and tedious.)

Murray State University

Accredited Bachelor of Independent Studies with a minimum of one day on campus.

Center for Continuing Education
Murray, KY 42071

Telephone: (502) 762-4150
Fax: (502) 762-3413

Toll-free phone: —
Year established: 1922

Degree levels: Bachelor's
Key person: Dr. Anita Lawson
Accreditation: Accredited
Ownership status: Nonprofit, state
Residency: Short residency
Cost index: $

Fields of study or special interest:
Independent study in almost any academic field

Other information:
Murray State offers a Bachelor of Independent Studies through correspondence study, television, and contract learning courses, as well as experiential credits. Many weekend and evening classes are available.

Twenty-four of the 128 semester hours must be taken with Murray State. Departmental challenge exams are available in some fields. If the exam is passed, credit is awarded. All students must attend a day-long seminar, held on a Saturday in April, August, and December. Admission to the program is based on satisfactory completion of the seminar.

All students must earn credit in basic skills, humanities, science, social sciences, electives, and a study project. Murray State credit can be earned by attending on- or off-campus courses, with correspondence courses, by gaining life experience credit, and by televised courses. Murray State charges $50 for portfolio assessment, plus $5 for each credit hour awarded as a result.

National Technological University

Accredited Master's in engineering, computer science, management and related areas, by viewing televised courses locally.

700 Centre Avenue
Fort Collins, CO 80526

Telephone: (303) 484-6050   Toll-free phone: ——
Fax: (303) 484-0668   Year established: 1984

Degree levels: Master's
Key person: Dr. Lionel Baldwin
Accreditation: Accredited
Ownership status: Nonprofit, independent
Residency: Short residency
Cost index: $$$

Fields of study or special interest:

Computer engineering, computer science, electrical engineering, management, manufacturing systems engineering, materials science, and management of technology

Other information:

NTU offers a wide range of graduate courses and noncredit short courses in technological subjects. These are transmitted by satellite digital compressed video to 45 university campuses from Alaska to Florida, as well as to corporate, government and university work sites.

Working professionals and technical managers take the classes, often in "real time" (as they are being taught on the campuses), with telephone links to the classrooms. NTU offers M.S. degrees in computer engineering, computer science, electrical engineering, engineering management, hazardous waste management, health physics, management of technology, manufacturing systems engineering, materials science and engineering, software engineering, and special majors.

In addition, about 400 short courses are broadcast on the NTU Network each year.

Newport University

Unaccredited nonresident degrees at all levels, including law, entirely through home study.

2220 University Drive
Newport Beach, CA 92660

Telephone: (714) 756-8297
Fax: ——
Degree levels: Associate's, Bachelor's, Master's, Doctorate, Law
Key person: Dr. Ted Dalton
Accreditation: Unaccredited
Ownership status: Proprietary
Residency: Nonresident
Cost index: $$

Toll-free phone: (800) 345-3272
Year established: 1976

Fields of study or special interest:
Business administration, law, education, engineering, psychology, human behavior, religion, general studies (Associate's only)

Other information:
Newport offers an "Individualized Education Program" based on "Directed Independent Study." For every course the student is sent a syllabus which identifies each concept or idea considered to be of importance to that course and advises which text to use. It also includes "performance requirements"— how to prove to the student's faculty advisor that he or she understands the concepts of the course.

Each student is assigned a faculty member (educational facilitator) for each course with whom they keep in touch by mail and phone. A senior paper is required for the Bachelor's. A thesis is strongly recommended for the Master's but it may be waived and replaced by two courses. A dissertation is recommended for the Doctorate, but it may be replaced by three courses with approval of Dean. Students of the four-year bar preparation program qualify to take the California bar exam.

Credit is given for experiential learning at the undergraduate level only. Newport has representatives or branch offices in 15 countries. Original name: Newport International University.

Northwood Institute

Accredited Associate's and Bachelor of Business Administration with a total of seven days required on campus.

3225 Cook Road
Midland, MI 48640

Telephone: (517) 832-4411
Fax: (517) 832-9590

Toll-free phone: (800) 445-5873
Year established: 1959

Degree levels: Associate's, Bachelor's
Key person: Donald A. King
Accreditation: Accredited
Ownership status: Nonprofit, independent
Residency: Short residency
Cost index: $$$

Fields of study or special interest:

Associate's in 12 fields (including accounting, advertising, banking/finance, fashion merchandising, fire science); Bachelor of Business Administration in management, accounting, and three dual majors: management and automotive marketing, computer information, and marketing

Other information:

Bachelor of Business Administration students attend two three-day seminars on campus (focusing on "updating business management"). Some programs may require more on-campus coursework, e.g. computer classes that have labs. B.B.A. students write a thesis and take a comprehensive oral and written exam on campus as the last step in their program. The exam lasts for several hours and is based on questions provided to the students in advance. Credit is given for experiential learning, equivalency exams, and transfer credit (up to 144 credits).

Degree coursework can be completed through weekend college classes, open-book comprehensive examinations (students research answers to structured topics, questions, and exercises; suggested references are provided); project courses (selected courses are available on a project basis. After completing a project, the student writes a 25-30 page report); correspondence courses with a proctored exam; approved college courses at other colleges.

Northwood offers its external degree programs through campuses in Michigan, Cedar Hill, Texas, and West Palm Beach, Florida, plus 22 satellite centers in 10 other states.

Norwich University

Accredited Bachelor's and Master's through home study plus two nine-day on-campus sessions a year in Vermont.

Vermont College
College Street
Montpelier, VT 05602

Telephone: (802) 828-8500
Fax: (802) 828-8855

Toll-free phone: (800) 336-6794 (outside VT)
Year established: 1834

Degree levels: Bachelor's, Master's
Key person: Gregory Dunkling
Accreditation: Accredited
Ownership status: Nonprofit, independent
Residency: Short residency
Cost index: $$$

Fields of study or special interest:
Liberal studies, visual art, writing, art therapy

Other information:
Vermont College of Norwich University offers programs structured to allow students great latitude in designing their studies in conjunction with faculty mentors. The Adult Degree Program (B.A.), begun in 1963, features short residencies in Vermont (nine days every six months or one weekend a month) alternating with study at home. The faculty guide and support student work in the liberal arts, including psychology and counseling, literature and writing, management, and education.

Graduate studies may be pursued through four programs. The Graduate Program, started in 1969, offers self-designed studies in the humanities, arts, education, and social sciences including psychology and counseling. Regional meetings are held quarterly or monthly by program faculty. Students work with two advisors, a core faculty member who is responsible for a geographical region of the country and a field advisor, a local expert in the student's field of study. The M.A. in art therapy offers a 15-month program which includes summer residencies in Vermont. An M.F.A. in writing and M.F.A. in visual arts are possible through off campus programs with nine-day residencies twice a year in Vermont.

Nova University

Accredited Bachelor's, Master's and Doctorates largely through independent study, with occasional group meetings and seminars at various locations.

3301 College Avenue
Fort Lauderdale, FL 33314

Telephone: (305) 475-7300
Fax: (305) 476-1999

Toll-free phone: (800) 541-NOVA
Year established: 1964

Degree levels: Doctorate
Key person: Stanley E. Cross
Accreditation: Accredited
Ownership status: Nonprofit, independent
Residency: Short residency
Cost index: $$$$

Fields of study or special interest:

Education, administration, business, computer systems

Other information:

Nova University has one of the more nontraditional Doctoral programs ever to achieve regional accreditation. The typical student attends one group meeting a month (generally two or three days), plus two one-week residential sessions, and from three to six practicums which emphasize direct application of research to the work place. Total time is about three-and-a-half years.

The University also offers a Doctor of Arts in information science in which students use interactive computers. A major part of instruction in this program is over computer networks. Residential work is offered through colloquia in 23 states. Nova will consider offering the program in the continental United States wherever a cluster of 20 to 25 students can be formed.

Degrees are offered in educational administration, teacher education, business administration, including international management, public administration, computer studies, and information science.

Ohio University

Accredited Associate's and an inexpensive Bachelor of General Studies entirely through home study.

External Student Program
301 Tupper Hall
Athens, OH 45701

Telephone: (614) 593-2150
Fax: (614) 593-4229

Toll-free phone: (800) 444-2420
Year established: 1804

Degree levels: Associate's, Bachelor's
Key person: Rosalie Terrell
Accreditation: Accredited
Ownership status: Nonprofit, state
Residency: Nonresident
Cost index: $$

Fields of study or special interest:
Specialized studies

Other information:
The Bachelor of Specialized Studies (B.S.S.) degree can be earned entirely though nonresident study. The External Student Program provides a counseling and advising service, and also acts as a liaison in dealing with other university offices. Credit for the degree can come from assessment of prior learning experiences, correspondence courses, independent study projects, and courses on television.

In many correspondence courses, one can take the examination only. If passed, credit for the course is given. These exams can be administered anywhere in the world and must be supervised. Forty-eight quarter hours of credit must be completed after enrolling at Ohio.

At times (but not all times) the university has offered a College Program for the Incarcerated, at unusually low cost.

Oklahoma City University

Accredited Bachelor's degree through independent study, with a minimum time of 16 weeks, and one short visit to the campus.

Competency-Based Degree Program
N. W. 23rd at N. Blackwelder
Oklahoma City, OK 73106

Telephone: (405) 521-5265   **Toll-free phone:** ——
Fax: (405) 521-5264   **Year established:** 1901

Degree levels: Bachelor's
Key person: Melissa Lamke
Accreditation: Accredited
Ownership status: Nonprofit, state
Residency: Short residency
Cost index: $$$

Fields of study or special interest:
Many fields

Other information:
A Bachelor of Arts or Science degree can be earned by utilizing a combination of independent study, seminars, assessment of prior learning, and traditional courses. Each student must visit the campus to attend an Orientation Workshop. Additional campus visits may be necessary. The University makes clear that while the program may be suitable for some distance students, it does not meet the needs of others. An evaluation of each student's educational situation is necessary.

Students must be at least 25 years of age, and be able to visit the campus for an Orientation Workshop. Because the program involves a great deal of student/faculty interaction, more than one visit may be necessary. All students must be enrolled for at least 16 weeks before earning the degree. This program is not intended to be a correspondence school.

Credit can be earned through traditional classroom work, independent study, directed readings, experiential learning, or a combination of these methods. Each student works with a coordinator to determine the areas of study in which the student needs to gain competence, and also how best to fulfill the degree requirements.

Open Learning Fire Service Program

Accredited Bachelor's degree in fire service areas, through correspondence courses taken from any of seven universities and colleges.

FEMA National Fire Academy, Field Program
16825 South Seton Avenue
Emmitsburg, MD 21727

Telephone: (301) 447-1127   **Toll-free phone:** (800) 238-3358
Fax: ——   **Year established:** 1977

Degree levels: Bachelor's
Key person: Edward J. Kaplan
Accreditation: Accredited
Ownership status: Nonprofit, federal
Residency: Nonresident
Cost index: Varies with each school

Fields of study or special interest:
Fire administration, fire prevention technology

Other information:
Accredited Bachelor's degree in fire services areas, through independent study courses, sponsored by the Federal Emergency Management Agency (FEMA) and taken from any of seven universities and colleges. The program is offered through seven regional colleges (all accredited): Cogswell College (California), University of Cincinnati, Memphis State University, Western Oregon State College, The University of Maryland University College, Western Illinois University, and Empire State College. All work is done by independent study. Students are sent a course guide, required textbooks, and their assignments. They communicate with instructors by mail and telephone. Supervised exams can be taken locally.

All of the upper-level courses can be completed through independent study at WIU and ESC. The remaining schools offer some independent study courses outside of the OLFSP curriculum, but not many. Hence, one may have to earn credits elsewhere and transfer them to the OLFSP institution, but there are no on-campus requirements for any of the OLFSP institutions.

Open University

Accredited nonresident degrees at all levels, through home study, ostensibly for U.K. residents only.

Walton Hall
Milton Keynes, Buckinghamshire MK7 6AA
England

Telephone: (44-908) 274066   Toll-free Phone: ——
Fax: ——   Year established: 1971

Degree levels: Bachelor's, Master's, Doctorate
Key person: C. R. Batten
Accreditation: Accredited
Ownership status: Nonprofit, state
Residency: Nonresident
Cost index: $$

Fields of study or special interest:
Arts, education, mathematics, social science, science, technology and management studies

Other information:
England's highly innovative and largest nontraditional university has become the model for similar ventures worldwide, and is the largest distance education institution in the world. Degrees at all levels are offered through a combination of home study texts, radio and television programs, audio- and videocassettes, week-long seminars during the summer months, and home laboratory kits for science students. Credit is earned only by passing examinations. A Bachelor's degree can take anywhere from three to six years of part-time study; a Doctorate from three to nine years.

About 30 hours of broadcast material are transmitted each week on BBC radio and television. The Open University is increasing its use of cassette material. There are currently more than 75,000 undergraduate students and over 7,000 graduate students registered. In addition, more than 20,000 associate students are studying single courses for personal interest or professional updating.

Open University was started as an experiment in 1971, and has grown into the most elaborate correspondence school in the world. As at other British universities, credit is earned only by passing examinations. There is a strict requirement of United Kingdom residency. Despite this, more than a few students outside England are enrolled, using a convenience address in Britain. This practice is strictly forbidden.

Open University of Israel

Bachelor's degrees on completion of eighteen home study courses, given only in Hebrew.

U.S. office: American Friends of the Open University
330 West 58 Street, Suite 4A
New York, NY 10019

Telephone: (212) 713-1515
Telephone in Israel: 972 (3) 646-0460
Fax: ——

Toll-free phone: ——
Year established: 1974

Degree levels: Bachelor's
Key person: Registrar
Accreditation: Accredited
Ownership status: Nonprofit, independent
Residency: Nonresident
Cost index: $$

Fields of study or special interest:
Many fields

Other information:
Israel's first open university offers the Bachelor's degree on completion of 18 home study courses, given only in Hebrew. Each course consists of a home study kit, which may include written materials, laboratory equipment, simulation games, videotapes, etc. Each course requires 16 to 18 weeks to complete, with a 15- to 18-hour a week time commitment.

Courses are available in natural sciences, life sciences, social sciences, mathematics, computer science, education, international relations, Jewish studies, management, and humanities. Noncredit courses are also offered in management enrichment, computers, video production, and cultural enrichment. Study group formation is encouraged, and tutorial sessions are held in study centers throughout Israel. Former name: Everyman's University.

Open University of the Netherlands

Accredited degrees awarded solely by passing examinations. Most courses in Dutch; a small but growing number in English.

P. O. Box 2960
6401 DL Heerlen Netherlands

Telephone: (31-45) 76-2222
Fax: (31-45) 71-1486

Toll-free phone: ——
Year established: 1984

Degree levels: Bachelor's, Doctorate
Key person: Marga Winnubust
Accreditation: Accredited
Ownership status: Nonprofit, state
Residency: Nonresident
Cost index: $

Fields of study or special interest:

Law, economics, management and administration, technology, natural science, social sciences, cultural studies

Other Information:

The Netherlands' first nontraditional university offers a wide range of self-study courses in seven general fields. In this program, modeled on Britain's Open University, credit is earned solely by passing examinations, and tutoring is available in study centers around Holland, or by telephone anywhere in the world.

However, as their catalog puts it, "the language of the great majority of courses is, naturally, Dutch. As yet, only a few courses, or sections of courses, are available in English."

Ottawa University

Accredited Bachelor's and Master's degrees primarily through home study, with a few short visits to centers in Kansas, Arizona and Wisconsin.

10865 Grandview, Building 20
Overland Park, KS 66210

Telephone: (913) 451-1431
Fax: (913) 242-7429

Toll-free phone: (800) 255-6380
Year established: 1865

Degree levels: Bachelor's, Master's
Key person: Harold D. Germer
Accreditation: Accredited
Ownership status: Nonprofit, church
Residency: Short residency
Cost index: $$$

Fields of study or special interest:
Bachelor's in many fields, Master's in human resources

Other information:
The Ottawa University University campus in Ottawa, Kansas serves mostly "traditional" college-age students with residential campus programs. Three adult centers located in Kansas City, Milwaukee and Phoenix serve nontraditional students exclusively.

The school suggests that anyone wanting information on the adult centers should contact those centers directly:

Ottawa University Phoenix, 2340 W. Mission Lane, Phoenix, AZ 85021 (602) 371-1188.

Ottawa University Milwaukee, 300 N. Corporate Drive, Milwaukee, WI 53045, (414) 879-0200.

Credit can be earned from evening classes (four terms per year), credit by evaluation (CLEP, ACT/PEP, and DANTE exams, military training programs) assessment of prior learning by preparing a portfolio ($300 fee), summer sessions, and directed studies (individually scheduled courses) for individuals and small groups. Students can begin at any time and progress at their own speed.

Pennsylvania State University

Associate's degrees entirely by correspondence study.

128 Mitchell Building
University Park, PA 16802

Telephone: (814) 865-5403

Fax: ——

Toll-free phone: ——

Year established: 1855

Degree levels: Associate's
Key person: Diane Leos
Accreditation: Accredited
Ownership status: Nonprofit, state
Residency: Nonresident
Cost index: $$

Fields of study or special interest:
Business administration; dietetic food systems management; arts, letters, and sciences

Other information:
Although few Associate's degrees are listed in this book, this is one of the few nonresident degrees available from a major state university. The degrees are offered entirely through independent study, mostly through correspondence courses offered by Penn State.

The Letters, Arts and Sciences degree is a broad liberal arts program, with courses available in arts, sciences, social and behavioral sciences, composition, and speech. The dietetic degrees are for people currently working in the food departments of such facilities as hospitals and nursing homes.

Portland State University

Accredited M.B.A. through two evening classes a week anywhere in the Northwest that six or more students sign up, plus two short visits a year to Portland.

P.O. Box 751
Portland, OR 97207

Telephone: (503) 725-3000
Fax: (503) 725-4882

Toll-free phone: (800) 547-8887, ext. 4822
Year established: 1946

Degree levels: Master's
Key person: Katherine Novy
Accreditation: Accredited
Ownership status: Nonprofit, state
Residency: Short residency
Cost index: $$

Fields of study or special interest:
Business administration

Other information:
The degree is offered through Portland State's School of Extended Studies. The Statewide M.B.A. program is currently offered in 12 colleges, community colleges, local businesses, and corporate sites throughout Oregon, and one site in Washington. A new site can be established in a community if there are at least six students who plan to enroll in the program.

Classes meet two evenings a week. Students are also involved in a study group with others at their site. Students enroll in two courses per term. Students see and hear the same lectures as on-campus students. One week after a lecture is delivered on campus, Statewide M.B.A. students view the class on videotape. There is a toll-free phone number so students can communicate with faculty concerning coursework.

The program takes three years to complete. Students must go to the Portland State campus twice a year for special case study classes.

Prescott College

Accredited Bachelor's in management, psychology, and other areas by home study, with two weekends on campus in Arizona.

Adult Degree Program
220 Grove
Prescott, AZ 86301

Telephone: (602) 776-7116
Fax: (602) 776-0724

Toll-free phone: ——
Year established: 1966

Degree levels: Bachelor's
Key person: Lydia Mitchell
Accreditation: Accredited
Ownership status: Nonprofit, independent
Residency: Short residency
Cost index: $$$

Fields of study or special interest:
Management, counseling, teacher education, human services, individually designed liberal arts programs

Other information:
Prescott's Adult Degree Program offers a student-centered independent study format, using instructors from the student's home community. Students normally take two courses every three months, meeting weekly with local instructors wherever they live. (Prescott helps locate these instructors.)

Students must come to the college for a weekend orientation at the beginning of their program, and for an additional liberal arts seminar, also held on a weekend. Degree programs can be individually designed to meet students' goals. Entering students normally have a minimum of 30 semester hours of prior college work.

One year of enrollment with Prescott is required to earn the degree. Credit for prior college-level learning is given through writing a life experience portfolio.

Queens University

Bachelor of Arts in political studies, psychology, or German from a major Canadian university entirely through correspondence study.

Kingston, Ontario K7L 2N6 Canada

Telephone: (613) 545-2471
Fax: ——

Toll-free phone: ——
Year established: 1841

Degree levels: Bachelor's
Key person: Registrar
Accreditation: Accredited
Ownership status: Nonprofit, state
Residency: Nonresident
Cost index: $$

Fields of study or special interest:
German, political studies, psychology

Other information:
A Bachelor of Arts degree (15 courses in total) concentrating in German, political studies, or psychology can be completed entirely through correspondence. Study involves use of textbooks, tapes, and course notes written by instructors. Students submit assignments for grading and write final examinations under supervision at various centers worldwide.

Telephone contact with instructors is possible.

Other concentrations can be fulfilled by taking a combination of correspondence courses through Queens and by transferring "Queens-approved" courses from other universities to complete degree requirements.

Regis University

Accredited Bachelor's and Master's in a university without walls program requiring a few one- or two-day visits to the campus.

3333 Regis Boulevard.
Denver, CO 80221

Telephone: (303) 458-3530
Fax: (303) 458-4129

Toll-free phone: (800) 727-6399 for UWW
Year established: 1877

Degree levels: Bachelor's, Master's
Key persons: J. Stephen Jacobs (Bachelor's), Robert Finkelmeier, Joan Buckley
Accreditation: Accredited
Ownership status: Nonprofit, church
Residency: Short residency
Cost index: $$$$

Fields of study or special interest:

Bachelor's in many fields, Master's in psychology, education, social sciences, or language and communication

Other information:

In a university without walls program, adults can complete a Bachelor of Arts degree in almost any field, earn Colorado or Wyoming teacher certification, and/or a Master of Arts degree in Liberal Studies through an individualized program of study in their home communities.

Students seeking a Bachelor's degree and/or teacher certification may design a program of study which includes transfer credit from other regionally accredited colleges and universities, guided independent study, internships, workshops, seminars, credit by examination, and credit by assessment of experiential learning.

Master's degree students may concentrate their study in one of four areas: psychology, education, social sciences, or language and communication. Study for the Master's degree includes guided independent study and interactive seminars held once per semester.

Students may combine study for the Master's degree with Colorado or Wyoming teacher certification.

Roger Williams University

Accredited Associate's and Bachelor's in engineering, writing, technology, and other fields, largely through nonresident study.

The Open Program
Old Ferry Road
Bristol, RI 02809

Telephone: (401) 254-3530
Fax: (401) 254-0490

Toll-free phone: ——
Year established: 1945

Degree levels: Associate's, Bachelor's
Key person: William Dunfey
Accreditation: Accredited
Ownership status: Nonprofit, independent
Residency: Short residency
Cost index: $$$

Fields of study or special interest:
Industrial technology, business administration, public administration, administration, administration of justice, and historic preservation

Other information:
The program assesses prior learning experiences. Assessment takes two to five months, and there is no extra charge for it. Credit is given for military training, CLEP and other exams, and prior college attendance.

Students earn credit by enrolling in external courses; independent studies; internships; and day, evening, summer, and special classroom courses. Credit can also be earned through courses from other schools, guided instruction by mail and telephone, videotapes, and other instructional packages.

Roosevelt University

Accredited Bachelor of General Studies entirely through external studies.

430 South Michigan Avenue
Chicago, IL 60605

Telephone: (312) 341-3866
Fax: (312) 341-3655

Toll-free phone: ——
Year established: 1945

Degree levels: Bachelor's
Key person: Gary K. Wolfe
Accreditation: Accredited
Ownership status: Nonprofit, independent
Residency: Nonresident
Cost index: $$$

Fields of study or special interest:
General studies

Other information:
People over 25 can earn the Bachelor of General Studies degree entirely by completing modules supplied by the University. A module comprises texts and other materials, representing a portion of a given course. Typically three modules make up one course. Most courses require examinations which can be taken either on campus or, by arrangement, near the student's home, supervised by a proctor.

At least 30 semester units must be completed after enrollment at Roosevelt.

Saint Joseph's College

Accredited Bachelor's and Master's requiring two or three weeks on campus, including a Professional Arts degree for registered nurses only.

Windham, ME 04069

Telephone: (207) 892-7841
Fax: (207) 892-7480

Toll-free phone: (800) 752-4723
Year established: 1912

Degree levels: Associate's, Bachelor's, Master's, certificates
Key person: Patricia M. Sparks
Accreditation: Accredited
Ownership status: Nonprofit, church
Residency: Short residency
Cost index: $$

Fields of study or special interest:
Health care administration, business administration, professional arts, long-term care, radiologic technology and management

Other information:
Three certificate and six degree programs are offered through Faculty Directed Independent Study with campus based advising and instruction. Certificates in health care management, long term care administration, and business administration. Associate of Science in management. Bachelor of Science in health care administration (with majors in general health care and long term care), Bachelor of Science in business administration, Bachelor of Science in professional arts (a degree completion program for licensed health care professionals), Bachelor of Science in radiologic technology (a degree completion program for rad techs.). A three week residency is required on the campus in Windham, Maine. A Master's in Health Services Administration is offered in the same format with a two week residency.

Instruction is provided through standard textbooks plus a study guide including a syllabus and course assignments. Personal instruction and assistance is available from faculty over a toll-free telephone line. Most courses require proctored examinations, which may be taken locally.

Saint Mary-of-the-Woods College

Accredited Bachelor's for women only in many fields and Master's in pastoral theology for women or men, with a week or less on campus each year.

Women's External Degree Program
Saint Mary-of-the-Woods, IN 47876

Telephone: (812) 535-5106   Toll-free phone: (800) 926-SMWC
Fax: (812) 535-4613   Year established: 1840

Degree levels: Bachelor's, Master's
Key person: Kathi Anderson
Accreditation: Accredited
Ownership status: Nonprofit, church
Residency: Short residency
Cost index: $$

Fields of study or special interest:
Many fields

Other information:
This old Catholic school offers its degrees through independent study, with a visit of a few days to campus each five-month term. Students may live anywhere in the world, except for education majors who must live within 400 miles of the college.

Majors offered at Bachelor's level include accounting, business administration, management, marketing, English, humanities, journalism, gerontology, paralegal studies, psychology, social science, theology, early childhood education, elementary education, kindergarten/primary education, and secondary education certification. The Master degrees is offered only in pastoral theology.

Life experience credit awarded to those with college-level knowledge acquired other than in a classroom environment. Excellent student support services are provided. Students are guided by faculty via mail and phone in off-campus independent study, punctuated with brief on-campus residencies (an average of one day per semester). Only women are awarded Associate's or Bachelor's degrees, but women and men can earn the Master's degree.

Saybrook Institute

Accredited Master's and Doctorates in psychology and human science through home study, with two weeks a year in San Francisco.

1550 Sutter Street
San Francisco, CA 94109

Telephone: (415) 441-5034
Fax: (415) 441-7556

Toll-free phone: ——
Year established: 1970

Degree levels: Master's, Doctorate
Key person: Kathy Trimble
Accreditation: Accredited
Ownership status: Nonprofit, independent
Residency: Short residency
Cost index: $$$

Fields of study or special interest:
Psychology, human science

Other information:
Courses are offered in an independent study format: a course guide is provided, specifying the required readings and including written lecture materials prepared by the faculty. Students may design their own courses as well. Student work focuses within four areas of concentration: clinical inquiry, systems inquiry, health studies, and consciousness studies. All students must attend a five-day planning seminar in San Francisco, and two one-week national meetings each year.

The "At-a-distance" learning format uses learning guides prepared by faculty for each course. Students complete coursework at home. Guides outline expectations of the course, and include written lecture materials prepared by the faculty, as well as reading materials. Progress is guided by communication with faculty by telephone, mail, and computer. Students may design their own courses as well.

Degrees can take from two to four years to complete. The Master's program is not a terminal program; it is designed to be stepping stone to the Ph.D.

Many well-known psychologists are associated with Saybrook (Rollo May, Stanley Krippner, Richard Farson, Nevitt Stanford, Clark Moustakas, etc.). Saybrook, until 1982, was called the Humanistic Psychology Institute.

(I should acknowledge that Saybrook asked to be taken out of this book, because they do not approve of certain other schools included in the book, and that I respectfully decline their request.)

Skidmore College

Accredited Bachelor's and Master's degrees in many subjects by home study, with three one-day visits to the campus.

University Without Walls
Saratoga Springs, NY 12866

Telephone: (518) 584-5000   **Toll-free phone:** ——
Fax: (518) 584-3023   **Year established:** 1911

Degree levels: Bachelor's
Key person: Dr. Robert H. Van Meter (Bachelor's); Dr. Lawrence Ries (Master's)
Accreditation: Accredited
Ownership status: Nonprofit, independent
Residency: Short residency
Cost index: $

Fields of study or special interest:
More than 50 Bachelor's majors; Master's in interdisciplinary studies

Other information:
Skidmore is one of the pioneers of the nontraditional movement, having offered a university without walls program since 1970. It is possible to earn their Bachelor of Arts or Bachelor of Science with a total of three days on campus: one for an admissions interview, a second for advising and planning, and the third to present a degree plan to a faculty committee.

Skidmore makes it clear that they hold their graduates to "standards of knowledge, competence and intellectual attainment which are no less comprehensive and rigorous than those established by traditional . . . programs." In addition to fulfilling all other requirements in the degree plan each student completes a final project demonstrating competence in his or her field.

Students can major in any of the dozens of fields offered by Skidmore or, with the assistance of faculty advisors, devise a self-determined major. In 1992 Skidmore launched a Master's program in interdisciplinary studies, modeled on its highly successful undergraduate program.

Southeastern University

Accredited Associate's and Bachelor's degrees by home study with two or four weeks on campus in Washington.

Distance Learning Degree Program
501 Eye Street SW
Washington, DC 20024

Telephone: (202) 488-8162
Fax: (202) 488-8093

Toll-free phone: ——
Year established: 1879

Degree levels: Associate's, Bachelor's
Key person: William H. Sherrill
Accreditation: Accredited
Ownership status: Nonprofit, independent
Residency: Short residency
Cost index: $$$

Fields of study or special interest:
Business management and accounting

Other information:
The Associate's degree can be earned on completion of 20 courses completed over five terms through correspondence study plus two weeks on the campus in Washington. The Bachelor's degree requires exactly twice as much work, and two two-week sessions on campus. Credit is available for prior coursework, various equivalency examinations, and life or work experience.

Instruction is provided through student-faculty communication by mail and telephone, and various tests, as well as the intensive on-campus weeks.

Southern California University for Professional Studies

Unaccredited nonresident Associate's, Bachelor's and Master's in business subjects.

202 Fashion Lane
Tustin, CA 92680

Telephone: (714) 832-0627
Fax: ——

Toll-free phone: (800) 477-2254
Year established: 1978

Degree levels: Associate's, Bachelor's, Master's
Key person: Betsy Burkman
Accreditation: Unaccredited
Ownership status:
Residency: Nonresident
Cost index: $$

Fields of study or special interest:
Business, management, marketing, health care administration, internal relations

Other information:
The degrees offered by home study are the Associate of Arts with a concentration in general studies, business, or paralegal studies; the Bachelor of Business Administration with a concentration in marketing, management, or accounting; and the Master of Business Administration. Also available are M.B.A.s with specializations in health care administration or internal relations. Courses are offered by mail, phone, and audiotape. Each course may be completed in four to 16 weeks. For the A.A. degree a minimum of five courses must be completed through the University. For either the Bachelor's or Master's, 10 courses (40 units) must be completed through the University. Undergraduate credit is given for other college work, vocational and business school courses, business training, seminars, and military service. Credits for work and life experience and prior learning is available for the Associate's and Bachelor's program.

A faculty mentor is available to assist each student. The student receives a study guide for each course (textbooks are not included, but can be either borrowed or purchased from the bookstore). The study guides include course information, chapter assignments and due dates, summaries of textbooks, instructors comments, etc. The student is encouraged to keep in touch with professors by mail and phone in order to get feedback and guidance as needed. Most courses include written assignments, a term paper or project.

Southwest University

Unaccredited Bachelor's, Master's, and Doctorates in many fields entirely through home study.

2200 Veterans Boulevard
Kenner, LA 70062

Telephone: (504) 468-2900
Fax: ——

Toll-free phone: (800) 433-5923
Year established: 1982

Degree levels: Bachelor's, Master's, Doctorate
Key person: Reg Sheldrick, Ph.D.
Accreditation: Unaccredited
Ownership status: Proprietary
Residency: Nonresident
Cost index: $$

Fields of study or special interest:
Business administration, psychology, counseling, hypnotherapy, education, hospital administration, health services administration, criminal justice, security administration, computer science, construction management, and engineering management

Other information:
Southwest University was established in 1982 by its president, Dr. Grayce Lee, and Dr. Reg Sheldrick. (Sheldrick also established the school now called Newport University.) Southwest University maintains a curriculum development office in Omaha, Nebraska.

Degree requirements can be satisfied by credit earned at other colleges and universities, credit given for military service/courses, credit for specialized training and experiential learning, and by undertaking independent study courses. All students must complete a final written project: term paper, thesis, dissertation, or research paper.

Southwestern Adventist College

Accredited Associate's and Bachelor's degrees in many fields with 11 days on campus the first year, three the second.

Keene, TX 76059

Telephone: (817) 556-4705
Fax: (817) 556-4744

Toll-free phone: (800) 433-2240
Year established: 1893

Degree levels: Bachelor's
Key person: Dr. Marie Redwine
Accreditation: Accredited
Ownership status: Nonprofit, church
Residency: Short residency
Cost index: $$$

Fields of study or special interest:
Business, communication, education, English, office administration, computer science, religion, social science, and history

Other information:
B.A., B.S., and Bachelor of Business Administration through the Adult Degree Program (ADP). Virtually all work can be completed at a distance, following an eight-day admission seminar, held each March, June, and October. Credit is earned by transfer of credit, proficiency exams, credit for prior learning (portfolio), and independent study by mail, computer, and telephone.

There are correspondence courses, in which students mail in their papers. Instructors are available by mail and phone. Credit may also be earned by television courses and classes at another school if approved by the faculty.

ADP students pay 80 percent of the tuition paid by on-campus students.

State University System of Florida

Accredited Bachelor's degrees with a minimum of two weeks on campus.

University of South Florida, External Degree Program
School of Extended Studies and Learning Technologies
4202 Fowler Avenue
Tampa, FL 33620

Telephone: (813) 974-4058   Toll-free phone: —
Fax: —   Year established: 1956

Degree levels: Bachelor's
Key person: Dr. Kevin Kearney
Accreditation: Accredited
Ownership status: Nonprofit, state
Residency: Short residency
Cost index: $$$ (Florida residents: $$)

Fields of study or special interest:
Independent studies; no majors offered

Other information:
The State University System of Florida External Degree Program is coordinated through the University of South Florida, and is accessible to students at three other schools: Florida State University (Tallahassee), University of Florida (Gainesville), and the University of North Florida (Jacksonville). The degree is awarded by University of South Florida.

The program is based on a curriculum of interdisciplinary studies, divided into four study areas: social sciences, natural sciences, humanities, and interarea studies. Pre-enrollees take a series of diagnostic tests to determine knowledge and skills. This information is used as guide for where to start in curriculum. Guided independent study (the tutorial) represents 90 percent of effort in first three study areas. Students receive an official guide which consists of learning objectives, concept inventories, and reading suggestions for each area (also a "study model" to illustrate how one might proceed). Students interact with a faculty advisor who monitors learning activities until such time as the advisor indicates that student is ready to sit for a comprehensive exam in that area.

There is a two-week on-campus seminar required for each area, although each of the first three areas can be waived if there is sufficient prior experience. A thesis is necessary as part of fourth study area.

Stephens College

Accredited Bachelor's degrees by home study, requiring two weekends or one week on campus.

College Without Walls
Campus Box 2083
Columbia, MO 65215

Telephone: (314) 876-7125
Fax: (314) 876-7248

Toll-free phone: (800) 388-7579
Year established: 1833

Degree levels: Associate's, Bachelor's
Key person: LuAnna Andrews
Accreditation: Accredited
Ownership status: Nonprofit, independent
Residency: Short residency
Cost index: $$$

Fields of study or special interest:
Many fields

Other information:
Students attend a three-semester-hour introductory liberal studies seminar at Stephens College prior to admission. The course is offered in seven-day or double weekend formats several times throughout the year. A minimum of 30 semester hours must be completed with Stephens College faculty. The College Without Walls is open to women and men 23 years of age and older. Degrees offered are the Bachelor of Arts, Bachelor of Science, and Associate in Arts.

The B.A. is available in business, psychology (clinical counseling or general), philosophy and religion, health care and a second area, allied health and a second area, philosophy, law and rhetoric, liberal arts, and student-initiated majors combining two or more disciplines. The B.S. is offered in health information management as well as early childhood and elementary education.

Degree requirements can be met through independent study. Independent study consists either of guided study (structured course, with syllabus, texts, and assignments) or contract study (student and faculty member [sponsor] design course objectives and content, method of evaluation, amount of credit, and course level). Students may also earn credits through other formats: short-term, intensive, on-campus courses; CLEP examinations; prior learning portfolios; courses transferred on admission; approved courses taken locally; and American Council on Education (ACE) evaluations.

Summit University

Unaccredited Bachelor's, Master's, and Doctorates entirely through home study.

7508 Hayne Boulevard
New Orleans, LA 70126

Telephone: (504) 241-0227   **Toll-free phone:** ——
Fax: (504) 243-1243   **Year established:** 1988

Degree levels: Bachelor's, Master's, Doctorates, Law
Key person: Melvin Suhd
Accreditation: Unaccredited
Ownership status: Nonprofit, religious
Residency: Nonresident
Cost index: $$

Fields of study or special interest:
Many fields

Other information:
Summit University declares that they are an "assessment university, critically assessing a person's lifelong learning." In other words, they assess a student's learning rather than teaching him or her anything. "No extraneous courses are required." (Summit does not offer courses.) Following an evaluation, the university determines how credits are to be earned. The student designs her or his own program with adjunct faculty or tutors from another school; the university does not have its own faculty per se. Students work with an RF/ACC (resource faculty/administrative academic counselor) in designing the program. Students can create their own degree category.

Each student has a trustee to work with throughout the process (to assess, advise, and counsel). The student (with assistance of the trustee) determines what is necessary to complete current studies. Students independently contract with outside mentors. Most learning is documented and credit is earned through writing papers and essays. A major study which adds to human knowledge is required at all degree levels.

After one has paid tuition for three years (two at the Master's level), no further tuition is required. The university central office is in its own small building in Louisiana, while the administrators work from their own offices around the country.

Syracuse University

Accredited Bachelor's, M.B.A., Master of Fine Arts (advertising, illustration), M.A. in food management, and more, with as little as three weeks on campus each year.

Independent Study Degree Programs
Syracuse, NY 13244

Telephone: (315) 443-3284
Fax: (315) 443-1954

Toll-free phone: —
Year established: 1870

Degree levels: Bachelor's, Master's
Key person: Robert Colley
Accreditation: Accredited
Ownership status: Nonprofit, independent
Residency: Short residency
Cost index: $$$

Fields of study or special interest:
Many fields

Other information:
A.A., B.A. in Liberal Studies, B.S. in business administration, criminal justice, or restaurant and food service management, Master of Arts in advertising design, or illustration, M.B.A., Master of Library Science, Master of Social Science, Master of Science in Nursing; all with short residency on campus, and independent study in between. All undergraduate degrees and the M.B.A. require three seven-day residencies per year.

The average completion time for the M.B.A. is $2\frac{1}{2}$ years; the Associate's and Bachelor's degrees take a minimum of one year (30 credits) for people with substantial transfer credit, though in practice most students take quite a bit longer. The Master of Social Science degree requires two 14-day sessions on campus in July (but not necessarily two consecutive sessions); alternative sessions are offered in Washington, D.C. and London. The M.A. degrees, which are taught by many of the country's best-known art directors, designers, and illustrators, require three two-week summer sessions on campus and several shorter sessions in New York, San Francisco, Chicago, and other metropolitan areas. The M.L.S. requires three two-week summer sessions, and four additional weeks over a two-year period. The M.S. in nursing requires four short summer sessions (one–three weeks each).

Thomas A. Edison State College

Accredited Associate's and Bachelor's in many fields, entirely by correspondence or home computer.

101 West State Street
Trenton, NJ 08608

Telephone: (609) 984-1100
Fax: (609) 984-1193

Toll-free phone: ——
Year established: 1972

Degree levels: Associate's, Bachelor's, (Master's?)
Key person: Jack Phillips, Registrar
Accreditation: Accredited
Ownership status: Nonprofit, state/local
Residency: Nonresident
Cost index: $

Fields of study or special interest:
119 fields of study

Other information:
Edison is one of the two most popular nontraditional colleges. (The other is the University of the State of New York.) Edison offers Associate's and Bachelor's degrees in business administration, applied science and technology, liberal arts, human services and nursing; 11 Associate and Bachelor's degrees in 119 areas of specialization.

Credit can be earned without any limitations through portfolio assessment (handbook available). It is possible to earn the degree entirely based on prior work, whether in college or not. Additional credit can be earned from Edison's own exams in dozens of subjects; guided study (correspondence courses using texts and videocassettes); courses by computer (many available through Edison's innovative CALL system: Computer Assisted Lifelong Learning); equivalency exams (over 400 available); military, business, and industry courses and training programs; credit for PONSI (Program on Non-collegiate Sponsored Instruction); television courses; credit for licenses and certificates, and transfer credit from accredited colleges. Courses can also be pursued over home computers through the Electronic University Network, described earlier in this book.

Academic advising is available to enrolled students over a toll-free number. Foreign students are welcome with certain restrictions. At press time, a Master's degree, long under development, was nearing completion.

Trinity University

Accredited Bachelor's degrees in many fields and a Master's in health care administration with a few days on campus each year.

715 Stadium Drive
San Antonio, TX 78212

Telephone: (512) 736-7011
Fax: (512) 736-7696

Toll-free phone: ——
Year established: 1869

Degree levels: Bachelor's, Master's
Key person: Richard C. Elliott
Accreditation: Accredited
Ownership status: Nonprofit, independent
Residency: Short residency
Cost index: $$$$

Fields of study or special interest:
Health care administration (Master's); many fields for Bachelor's

Other information:
The Bachelor's degree is offered through an Individualized Degree Program, in which students pursue independent study in dozens of subject areas. Students are provided with study units, which typically consist of books to be read, papers to be written, and sometimes an examination. Students are expected to consult with faculty four to six times each term (in person or by telephone).

The Master's in health care administration available almost entirely through home study. Each course begins with an intensive three-day on-campus program, followed by independent home study. Support is offered in the form of regular teleconferencing sessions with the instructor.

Troy State University

Accredited Associate's and Bachelor's degrees in business, history, political science, and the social sciences entirely through nonresident study.

P. O. Drawer 4419
Montgomery, AL 36103

Telephone: (205) 241-9553
Fax: (205) 670-3774

Toll-free phone: ——
Year established: 1887

Degree levels: Bachelor's
Key person: Dr. James R. Macey
Accreditation: Accredited
Ownership status: Nonprofit, state
Residency: Nonresident
Cost index: $$

Fields of study or special interest:

Resource management (business), English, history, political science, social science, and psychology

Other information:

The Bachelor of Arts or Science in professional studies and Associate of Science in general education can be earned through a combination of learning contracts with Troy State University in Montgomery (TSUM), TSUM television courses, transfer credit from and transient credit at other regionally accredited colleges/universities, and prior learning assessment (credit by examination; evaluation of previous training in the military, business and/or industry; and portfolio assessment). Majors are available in resource management (business), English, history, political science, social science, and psychology. Students must complete a minimum of 50 quarter hours under TSUM sponsorship for the Bachelor's degrees and 25 quarter hours for the Associate's degree.

Faculty have developed learning contracts that closely parallel requirements in University resident courses. They are available for most courses. Students may also design their own learning contracts with the guidance/assistance of Troy State faculty.

No correspondence courses are offered, but they can be taken at other schools for Troy State credit. Credit for life experience is available, but only after a student has completed a course in this subject.

Union Institute

A well-regarded accredited Ph.D. in many fields primarily (not entirely) by home study. Not fast; not inexpensive.

440 East McMillan Street
Cincinnati, OH 45206

Telephone: (513) 861-6400
Fax: (513) 651-2310

Toll-free phone: (800) 543-0366
Year established: 1964

Degree levels: Bachelor's, Doctorate
Key person: Dr. Jennifer King Cooper
Accreditation: Accredited
Ownership status: Nonprofit, independent
Residency: Short residency
Cost index: $$$$

Fields of study or special interest:
Many fields

Other information:
Union was established by the Union for Experimenting Colleges and Universities, a consortium including some large state universities, to be, in effect, their alternative program. The undergraduate university without walls Bachelor's degree may involve independent study, directed reading, internships, on-the-job education, classroom instruction, tutorials, etc., as well as credit for prior learning experiences. The required residency involves a weekend colloquium (held in various locations) and occasional seminars. At least nine months are required to earn the degree.

The Ph.D. begins with a 10-day "entry colloquium" held in various locations. The candidate develops a committee of at least five, including two peers, and works with them to establish a learning agreement, including an internship. All Ph.D. students must attend at least three five-day seminars at least six months apart, and another 10 days' worth of meetings with three or more other learners, or 35 days total. A typical Doctoral program takes two to four years.

Former name: Union Graduate School (until 1990).

Universidad de San Jose

Accredited Master's and Doctorates, in English, through independent study plus a two-week residency in Costa Rica.

Regional Information Office
7891 West Flagler Street, Suite 123
Miami, FL 33144

Telephone: (305) 225-3500
Fax: ——

Toll-free phone: ——
Year established: 1976

Degree levels: Master's, Doctorate
Key person: Johnny Ortega, M.B.A.
Accreditation: Accredited
Ownership status: Private, nonprofit
Residency: Short residency
Cost index: $$$

Fields of study or special interest:
Administrative sciences, education and humanities, psychology and behavioral science, social science, biological science, science

Other information:
The International Post-Graduate School has recently begun offering graduate degrees through nonresidential instruction, with a two week on-campus residency requirement. Students are able to complete their studies for a post-graduate degree off-campus under the direct guidance of an academic advisor. The Master's program must be completed in less than three years, the Doctorate in less than five. Two study options are offered: a Curriculum Based Program for students who have the need to take traditional coursework in addition to the thesis/dissertation, and a Research Based program for qualified students who already possess the theoretical knowledge and experience in their area of expertise.

The school is accredited by the government of Costa Rica.

University of Alabama, New College

Accredited Bachelor's in many fields with two days on campus, and a Master's in criminal justice with two weeks on campus.

External Degree Program
P. O. Box 870182
Tuscaloosa, AL 35487

Telephone: (205) 348-6000
Fax: (205) 348-6544

Toll-free phone: ——
Year established: 1831

Degree levels: Bachelor's, Master's
Key person: Dr. Harriet Cabell
Accreditation: Accredited
Ownership status: Nonprofit, state
Residency: Short residency
Cost index: $$

Fields of study or special interest:
Many fields

Other information:
The degrees of Bachelor of Arts or Bachelor of Science may be earned entirely through nonresident independent study with the exception of a two-day degree planning seminar on the campus at the start of the program. At least 32 semester hours of work must be completed after admission to the University. This can be by out-of-class contract learning, correspondence courses, television courses, Weekend College, prior learning evaluation, or on-campus courses at the university.

Interdisciplinary degrees are offered in human services, humanities, social sciences, natural sciences, applied sciences, administrative sciences, and communication. A 12-semester-hour senior project is required of all students. Academic advising and planning can be done by telephone.

There is a Master's in Criminal Justice, requiring two weeks on campus, offered through the College of Continuing Studies, Box 870388, Tuscaloosa, AL 35487-0388. There often seems to be a waiting list to get into the Master's program.

University of Durham

Accredited M.B.A. entirely through distance learning plus one week a year in residency at various locations.

Business School
Mill Hill Lane
Durham City, DH1 3LB England

Telephone: (44-91) 374-2219
Fax: (44-91) 374-3389

Toll-free phone: ——
Year established: 1988 (this program)

Degree levels: Master's
Key person: John F. Ross
Accreditation: Accredited
Ownership status: Nonprofit, state
Residency: Short residency
Cost index: $$$

Fields of study or special interest:
Business administration

Other information:
In mid-1988 Durham introduced a distance learning M.B.A. (they have offered a traditional M.B.A. since 1967). The program is administered by the University Business School to students in over 40 countries.

The three- to four-year course of study combines specially written distance-learning materials, annotated texts, audiotapes, and one week per year of intensive residential seminars (first year excluded). Examinations are required at regular intervals.

University of Evansville

Accredited Bachelor's degrees in many fields through home study plus a two-day on-campus workshop in Indiana.

Center for Continuing Education
1800 Lincoln Avenue
Evansville, IN 47722

Telephone: (812) 479-2981
Fax: (812) 479-2320

Toll-free phone: ——
Year established: 1854

Degree levels: Bachelor's
Key person: Lynn R. Penland
Accreditation: Accredited
Ownership status: Nonprofit, church
Residency: Short residency
Cost index: Varies

Fields of study or special interest:
Many fields

Other information:
The External Studies Program offers a B.A. or B.S. in virtually any field other than technical or professional areas, such as mathematics, chemistry, engineering, computer science, nursing, and education.

Work is completed through a combination of classroom and correspondence courses, coursework from nontraditional sources, proficiency exams, independent study, and credit for life experience learning. Students develop their own individualized plans in a two-day, on-campus educational planning workshop.

University of Idaho

Accredited Master of Science in engineering, computer science, and psychology entirely through home study plus one day on campus for a comprehensive examination.

Video Outreach Program
Janssen Engineering Building
Moscow, ID 83843

Telephone: (208) 885-6111

Fax: (208) 885-5752

Toll-free phone: (800) 824-2889

Year established: ——

Degree levels: Master's
Key person: Karyl Davenport
Accreditation: Accredited
Ownership status: Nonprofit, state
Residency: Nonresident
Cost index: $$

Fields of study or special interest:

Engineering (civil, computer, electrical, geological, mechanical), computer science, and psychology (human factors)

Other information:

Master's degrees in electrical, mechanical, civil and computer engineering, computer science, and psychology (human factors) are offered via the Video Outreach program.

The courses are offered by videocassette, with new lectures each year, mostly taped during the actual on-campus classes, then rushed to students, along with whatever written materials were distributed during class. Thus the classes offered to off-campus students are exactly the same as those done in residence.

Most examinations can be taken locally, under supervision, however all students must go to the campus at least once to take a final comprehensive examination or to defend a research thesis. Access to a computer is essential for many of the courses.

University of Iowa

Accredited Bachelor of Liberal Studies entirely through home study.

Center for Credit Programs
116 International Center
Iowa City, IA 52242

Telephone: (319) 335-2575
Fax: (319) 335-2740

Toll-free phone: (800) 272-6430
Year established: 1847

Degree levels: Bachelor's
Key person: Scot Wilcox
Accreditation: Accredited
Ownership status: Nonprofit, state
Residency: Nonresident
Cost index: $$

Fields of study or special interest:
Liberal studies

Other information:
The Bachelor of Arts in liberal studies can be earned entirely by correspondence from the University of Iowa. There are no majors in the program, but students must earn 12 credits in three of these five areas: humanities, communication and arts, science and math, social sciences, and professional fields (business, education, etc.). Credit is also earned through guided correspondence study courses.

Students mail in assignments and take proctored exams. Credit can also be earned through on-campus evening and weekend courses, televised courses, off-campus courses held at sites throughout Iowa, courses from other regionally accredited four-year colleges (both on-campus and correspondence), and telebridge courses. "Telebridge" is a statewide system of two-way audio conferencing which permits classes to be held at remote locations.

No credit is given for life experience. To qualify for admission, a student must live in the United States and have completed 62 transferable units or have an Associate's degree. At least 45 semester hours must be earned at the Iowa Regents Universities (University of Iowa, Iowa State University, University of Northern Iowa).

University of London

Accredited nonresident Bachelor's, Master's, and Doctorates and Law degrees in a variety of fields from the school that invented the whole concept.

Senate House, Malet Street
London WC1E 7HU England

Telephone: (44-71) 636-8000   Toll-free phone: ——
Fax: (44-71) 636-5894   Year established: 1836

Degree levels: Bachelor's, Master's, Doctorates, Law
Key person: Secretary for External Students
Accreditation: Accredited
Ownership status: Nonprofit, state
Residency: Nonresident
Cost index: $$

Fields of study or special interest:
Many fields

Other information:
London was the world's first external degree program and, after over a century and a half, it is still among the beStreet They do have an annoying policy that only holders of their own Bachelor's degree can enroll in M.Phil. or Ph.D. programs, but they offer an increasing number of degrees specifically geared to correspondence students. Five Master's degrees are recommended for distance-learning students: agricultural development, distance education, environmental management, and organizational behavior/occupational psychology. In classics, French, law, and most of the undergraduate programs, academic guidance is less extensive.

Courses are non-time-limited and students work at their own pace to complete an individualized program. Assessment is by examination and (for some degrees) by thesis. Examinations in the U.S. are administered by the Educational Testing Center in Princeton, New Jersey. Several independent correspondence schools offer nondegree preparation for London's exams, including the National Extension College (18 Brooklands Avenue, Cambridge CB2 2HN, U.K.), Rapid Results College (27-37 Street. George's Road, London SW19 4DS, U.K.), and Holborn College (200 Greyhound Road, London W14 9RY U.K.).

University of Maryland

Accredited Bachelor's degrees by home study or television courses, with a few short visits to the campus in Maryland.

University College
College Park, MD 20742

Telephone: (301) 985-7036
Fax: (301) 454-0399

Toll-free phone: (800) 888-UMEC
Year established: 1856

Degree levels: Bachelor's
Key person: Dr. Paul Hamlin
Accreditation: Accredited
Ownership status: Nonprofit, state
Residency: Short residency
Cost index: $$

Fields of study or special interest:
Technology & management, behavioral & social sciences, humanities, fire science

Other information:
University College, the continuing higher education campus of the University of Maryland System, offers B.A. and B.S. degrees in flexible formats through its Open Learning Program. Attendance is optional except for the introductory session and examinations. There are regional educational centers throughout the Washington-Baltimore area.

Some courses are offered over the Mind Extension University cable television channel. They can also be received by people with satellite dishes, or the videotapes can be purchased directly. A primary concentration in fire science is offered via independent study in a six-state region and the District of Columbia. Credit is available for relevant college-level prior learning.

University of Massachusetts at Amherst

Accredited Master's in engineering through television courses (by cable, satellite, or video-tape).

Video Instructional Program (VIP)
College of Engineering
113 Marcus Hall
Amherst, MA 01003

Telephone: (413) 545-0063
Fax: ——

Toll-free phone:——
Year established: 1863

Degree levels: Master's
Key person: Merilee Hill
Accreditation: Accredited
Ownership status: Nonprofit, state
Residency: Nonresident
Cost index: $$$

Fields of study or special interest:
Engineering management and electrical and computer engineering

Other information:
The Video Instructional Program (VIP) is a video-based program designed to meet the needs of working engineers. Students are able to enroll in and complete the very same courses that are offered on-campus, via videotape or satellite delivery. Students may enroll in semester-length courses as a graduate degree or nondegree student, audit courses, or take short non-credit courses.

Master of Science degrees are offered in engineering management and electrical and computer engineering.

University of Minnesota

Accredited nonresident Bachelor's degrees in many fields of study for people in Minnesota and nearby states and provinces.

Program for Individualized Learning
201 Westbrook Hall
Minneapolis, MN 55455

Telephone: (612) 624-4020
Fax: (612) 624-6369

Toll-free phone: ——
Year established: 1851

Degree levels: Bachelor's
Key person: Kent Warren
Accreditation: Accredited
Ownership status: Nonprofit, state
Residency: Nonresident
Cost index: $$

Fields of study or special interest:
Almost any field except business, education, engineering or computer science

Other information:
B.A. and B.S. degrees for students willing to take responsibility for designing and implementing their degree programs. The program (formerly called University Without Walls) offers no courses or exams of its own. Instead, it assists students in using resources at the University, at other institutions, and in the community. These might include local or correspondence courses, independent study projects, and assessment of prior learning. At least a year of study is required after admission.

Since there are no predesigned majors or prescribed curricula, each student develops an individualized degree plan. A set of standards, called graduation criteria, provide a framework for structuring and assessing degree programs. Requirements include an area of concentration, broad learning in the liberal arts, and a command of written English.

Programs are not available in general business administration, accounting, public school teaching, engineering, or computer science.

The Program serves students in Minnesota and adjacent states and Canadian provinces.

University of Missouri–Columbia

Accredited Bachelor's in general agriculture entirely through correspondence study.

College of Agriculture Food and Natural Resources
Nontraditional Study Program
215 Gentry Hall
Columbia, MO 65211

Telephone: (314) 882-6287
Fax: (314) 882-6957

Toll-free phone: ——
Year established: 1839

Degree levels: Bachelor's
Key person: Dr. Richard Linhardt
Accreditation: Accredited
Ownership status: Nonprofit, state
Residency: Nonresident
Cost index: $$

Fields of study or special interest:
Agriculture

Other information:
Bachelor of Science in general agriculture is awarded for at least 128 semester hours including required courses and electives. Options for earning credit include college course work, correspondence study, extension courses, CLEP, departmental examination, and evaluation of life learning experience. Only students who have not enrolled in any school full time for at least five years are accepted. Prior college-level work is required. Students with less than 60 hours of college work are discouraged.

The program is not available to persons outside the United States.

University of Oklahoma

Accredited Bachelor's and Master's in liberal studies, with a total of two to seven weeks on campus in Oklahoma.

College of Liberal Studies
1700 Asp Avenue, Suite 226
Norman, OK 73037

Telephone: (405) 325-1061
Fax: (405) 325-7605

Toll-free phone: (800) 522-4389
Year established: 1890

Degree levels: Bachelor's, Master's
Key person: Konnie Hall, Coordinator, Student Information
Accreditation: Accredited
Ownership status: Nonprofit, state
Residency: Short residency
Cost index: $$ (OK residents), $$$ (non-OK residents)

Fields of study or special interest:
Liberal studies

Other information:
The College of Liberal Studies was established in 1960, making it one of the pioneers in this field. There are no majors; students do elective study based on their interests. Work is done through a combination of guided independent study based on a faculty-student tutorial relationship and short-term intensive seminars on the University of Oklahoma campus.

Bachelor's students complete studies in four areas: humanities, natural sciences, social sciences, and a final area which integrates the previous three. Each area takes up to a year and is worth 30 units. Any or all of the first three areas can be waived, either based on prior study or by passing an examination. An option for people with two years of college begins with a five-day residential seminar, then completion of the first three phases in about a year, with one required seminar. The final seminar is the same as in the four-year program. Grading is based on comprehensive exams taken at college or locally, supervised by a proctor. The curriculum consists of core study from reading lists developed by the faculty, learning contracts allowing students to focus on a topic of particular interest, and a senior thesis.

The Master of Liberal Studies is largely for people with a specialized Bachelor's who wish a broader education. It requires two two-week seminars and one three-week colloquium on campus. The Master's program is based on an individualized study program/plan developed by the student and advisors, culminating in the writing and presentation of a thesis.

University of Phoenix

Accredited B.A., M.A., and M.B.A., either by using a personal computer, or through attending one-evening-a-week classes.

4615 East Elmwood Street
P.O. Box 52069
Phoenix, AZ 85072

Telephone: (602) 966-7400
Fax: (602) 829-9030

Toll-free phone: (800) 888-4935
Year established: 1976

Degree levels: Bachelor's, Master's
Key person: Dr. Sheila Murphy
Accreditation: Accredited
Ownership status: Proprietary
Residency: Nonresident
Cost index: $$$$

Fields of study or special interest:
Management, business administration, organizational management

Other information:
The B.S. in business administration is the equivalent of the last two years of undergraduate college, and may be completed by using a personal computer. Courses are taken one at a time, spread out over two years.

The M.B.A. consists of 14 courses, offered one at a time over a six-week period, spread out over two years. Courses may either be taken residentially at centers throughout the west, or nonresidentially by use of a personal computer. Students can use the computer to interact with other students and with faculty, to receive and submit assignments, etc.

The M.A. in Management is comparable in scope and approach to the M.B.A., but the courses are focused more on human resources management.

University of Santa Barbara

Unaccredited Master's and Doctorates in business and education through home study plus three weeks in Santa Barbara.

4050 Calle Real #200
Santa Barbara, CA 93110

Telephone: (805) 569-1204
Fax: (805) 967-6289

Toll-free phone: ——
Year established: 1973

Degree levels: Master's, Doctorate
Key person: Dr. Julia Reinhart Coburn
Accreditation: Unaccredited
Ownership status: Nonprofit, independent
Residency: Short residency
Cost index: $$

Fields of study or special interest:
Education, business administration. human behavior, international studies

Other information:
M.A. and Ph.D. in education, M.B.A., M.S. in business administration, international business, and a number of business-related fields. All courses of study contain an international studies component and an ethics emphasis. The programs all require a minimum residency of three weeks in Santa Barbara, for intensive seminars preparatory to self-guided research. The resident faculty and nonresident advisors all have traditional Doctorates.

Degree candidates must complete courses and independent study work, and pass an examination in each study area.

Originally established in Florida as Laurence University. Accredited by PASC, the Pacific Association of Schools and Colleges, an unrecognized but legitimate accrediting agency which is in the process of applying for recognition by the Department of Education.

University of Sarasota

Accredited programs offering the M.B.A. and Doctorates in education by home study plus six weeks in Florida.

5250 17th Street, Suite 3
Sarasota, FL 34235

Telephone: (813) 379-0404
Fax: (813) 379-9464

Toll-free phone: (800) 331-5995
Year established: 1969

Degree levels: Master's, Doctorate
Key person: Richard T. Adams, Ph.D.
Accreditation: Accredited
Ownership status: Nonprofit, independent
Residency: Short residency
Cost index: $$$

Fields of study or special interest:
Business, education

Other information:
Master of Business Administration, Master of Arts in education, and Doctor of Education. Some intensive coursework in Florida is required. Courses are in the summer, with one-week seminars in winter and spring. Total residency may be as short as six weeks.

The university's programs consist of seminars and supervised individual research and writing, combined with the residential sessions. Master's candidates either write a thesis or complete a directed independent study project. Doctoral students must write a dissertation. Many of the students are teachers and school administrators.

The university was originally known as Laurence University, the predecessor of the Laurence University that opened in California and is now the University of Santa Barbara.

University of South Africa

Accredited nonresident Bachelor's, Master's and Doctorates in many fields from the largest correspondence university in the English-speaking world.

P.O. Box 392, Muckleneuk Ridge
Pretoria 0001 South Africa

Telephone: (27-12) 429-2555	Toll-free phone: ——
Fax: (27-12) 429-2565	Year established: 1910

Degree levels: Bachelor's, Master's, Doctorate
Key person: Registrar
Accreditation: Accredited
Ownership status: Nonprofit, state
Residency: Nonresident
Cost index: $

Fields of study or special interest:
Many fields

Other information:
UNISA offers Bachelor's, Master's, and Doctorates entirely by correspondence. Examinations are taken at South African embassies and consulates worldwide. Degrees at all levels are offered in arts, science, law, theology, education, and economic and management sciences through a technique called "tele-tuition," using course materials, tapes, slides, etc.

A minimum of 10 courses is required for the Bachelor's degree, which takes a minimum of three years to complete. The government-subsidized program is relatively inexpensive. Before registering, one must obtain a Certificate of Full or Conditional Exemption from the South African Matriculation Examination, obtained from the Matriculation Board, P.O. Box 3854, Pretoria, South Africa 0001. People worldwide are admitted. Syllabi and course descriptions are available free of charge from the registrar.

Note: A reader who has mastered the intricacies of dealing with UNISA has written a very helpful, detailed 110-page manual on how to do it. For information, write to South Africa Information, 23400 Covello Street, West Hills, California 91304.

University of Surrey

An accredited British Master's in education entirely through completion of home-study modules.

Department of Educational Studies
Guildford
Surrey, GU2 5XH England

Telephone: (44-483) 300-800
Fax: (44-483) 300-803

Toll-free phone: ——
Year established: ——

Degree levels: Master's
Key person: Mrs. Elizabeth Oliver
Accreditation: Accredited
Ownership status: Nonprofit, state
Residency: Nonresident
Cost index: $$

Fields of study or special interest:
Education

Other information:
Surrey offers a distance-learning M.S. in education "designed for educators and human resource personnel in all forms of post-compulsory education and training." The full course consists of eight "modules," plus a research dissertation. Each module takes about three months to complete, so it is possible to finish the M.S. in three years, although students are allowed six years.

As only two of the 25 possible modules require face-to-face workshops, most students will have no trouble completing the degree by correspondence alone. There are no examinations.

University of the State of New York

Accredited Bachelor of Arts and Bachelor of Science entirely through nonresidential study at Regents College, part of America's oldest chartered state university.

Regents College
1450 Western Avenue
Albany, NY 12203

Telephone: (518) 474-3703   Toll-free phone: ——
Fax: (518) 485-7520   Year established: 1784

Degree levels: Bachelor's
Key person: C. Wayne Williams, Executive Director
Accreditation: Accredited
Ownership status: Nonprofit, private
Residency: Nonresident
Cost index: $

Fields of study or special interest:
Business, liberal arts, nursing, and technology

Other information:
B.A. and B.S. by nonresidential study. The largest and, along with Thomas A. Edison State College, the most popular nonresident degree program in the U.S. Part of the oldest educational agency in America, the University of the State of New York, Regents College has no campus and offers no courses of its own. It evaluates work done elsewhere, and awards its own degrees to persons who have accumulated sufficient units, by a broad variety of means. Credit for nonduplicative college courses (both classroom and distance) and many noncollege learning experiences (company courses, military, etc.) evaluated as college-level.

Regents College recognizes many equivalency exams and offers its own as well, given nationwide and, by arrangement, at foreign locations. Each degree has its own faculty-established requirements with regards to areas of emphasis, but they are not restrictive. The program is described in brochures and catalogs, sent free to all who request them. If nonschool learning experiences cannot be assessed easily at a distance, or by exam, the student may go to Albany, New York, for an oral examination.

Regents College makes available to enrolled students a service called DistanceLearn, which is a computer database of nearly 7,000 proficiency examinations and courses offered by other schools that can be completed through home study.

University of Wales

Accredited Doctorates mostly by home study, with short visits to Wales from time to time.

University Registry, Cathays Park
Cardiff CF1 3NS Wales, United Kingdom

Telephone: (44-222) 22656

Fax: ——

Toll-free phone: ——

Year established: ——

Degree levels: Master's, Doctorate
Key person: Registrar
Accreditation: Accredited
Ownership status: Nonprofit, state
Residency: Short residency
Cost index: $

Fields of study or special interest:
Many fields

Other information:
External Ph.D.s may be pursued at any of the campuses of the university. Each candidate works with a supervisor, who is a present or former full-time member of the academic staff. An applicant must have an approved Bachelor's degree, demonstrate that there are adequate facilities at the "home base" for pursuing research (library, laboratory, archives, etc.), and be able to pay regular visits to the university (typically three visits a year to meet with the director of studies, or one month a year in continuous work).

The student's employer must confirm that the student will be working (full or part time) on a research topic. A supervisor is also appointed at the place of employment. After the dissertation is read, there is an oral examination, following which either the degree is granted, the student is asked to modify the dissertation, or the degree is refused. If the student can only pursue the necessary dissertation research part-time, then he or she must be enrolled for 15 terms instead of nine, but the other rules remain the same.

Initial inquiries should be directed to the department head of the relevant department, or the registrar of the institution chosen. They are: University College of Wales, Aberystwyth, Dyfed SY23 2AX; University College of North Wales, Bangor, Gwynedd LL57 2DG; University of Wales College, Cathays Park, Cardiff CF1 3XA; University College of Swansea, Singleton Park, Swansea SA2 8PP; Saint David's University College, Lampeter, Dyfed SA48 7ED; University of Wales, College of Medicine, Heath Park, Cardiff CF4 4XN.

.iversity of Warwick

Accredited British M.B.A. largely through home study, with three eight-day sessions on campus in England or Hong Kong.

Distance Learning MBA Program
Warwick Business School
Coventry CV4 7AL England

Telephone: (44-203) 524-100   Toll-free phone:——
Fax:——   Year established: 1965

Degree levels: Master's
Key person: Dr. Roy Johnston
Accreditation: Accredited
Ownership status: Nonprofit, state
Residency: Short residency
Cost index: $$$

Fields of study or special interest:
Business administration

Other information:
Students anywhere in the world may register with Warwick, and then pursue the M.B.A. from home. Students are required to attend an eight-day seminar at Warwick (or at the Hong Kong office) each September, before beginning each of three parts of program. Optional weekend seminars are held at Warwick, Hong Kong, Malaysia, and Singapore three times a year. Access to a computer is recommended but not essential.

The main work is completing assignments at the rate of two per month. Each student is assigned a tutor for each course who corrects work and is available by phone. Tutors come from the Warwick staff or "another institution of higher education." Exams are held regularly at Warwick, Hong Kong, and Singapore. Special arrangements can be made for exams in other countries. (Exams are held in as many as 30 countries each year.)

The program has three parts. Parts A and B cover core ideas and "tools" needed in business. Part C gives the student a choice of electives, to go in depth in area of interest. At end of A, B, & C, a dissertation is written.

The period of study is normally four years, roughly 12 hours a week, but it can be three years if the dissertation is completed during the final year of study.

University of Waterloo

Accredited Bachelor's degrees entirely through home study, for people in Canada and the U.S.

Correspondence Office
Waterloo, Ontario N2L 3G1 Canada

Telephone: (519) 888-4050
Fax:——

Toll-free phone: ——
Year established: 1957

Degree levels: Bachelor's
Key person: Bruce A. Lumsden
Accreditation: Accredited
Ownership status: Nonprofit, state
Residency: Nonresident
Cost index: $

Fields of study or special interest:
Many fields

Other information:
Bachelor's degrees can be earned entirely through correspondence. They include a non-major B.A., a B.A. with a major in classical studies, economics, English, geography, history, philosophy, psychology, religious studies, or social development studies; a Bachelor of Environmental Studies in geography; and a non-major B.Sc. in science. Credit is considered for prior academic experience, but no credit is given for experiential learning.

The programs are available to people residing in Canada and the United States, but U.S. citizens pay three to four times the tuition of Canadian citizens. All courses are offered on a rigid time schedule, in which papers and exams must be done by very specific times. As a result, there have been postal delivery problems with some U.S. students. (Suggestion: there is a maximum of six assignments per course; it might well be worth the expense of sending them in via Federal Express or fax.)

University of Wisconsin–Madison

A post-Bachelor's Professional Development Degree in engineering entirely by correspondence study.

College of Engineering
432 North Lake Street
Madison, WI 53706

Telephone: (608) 262-0133
Fax: ——

Toll-free phone: ——
Year established: 1849

Degree levels: Certificates
Key person: Cheri McKentley
Accreditation: Accredited
Ownership status: Nonprofit, state
Residency: Nonresident
Cost index: $$

Fields of study or special interest:
Engineering

Other information:
The Professional Development Degree program in engineering may be earned through correspondence and independent study or one can combine them with coursework from local accredited universities. The Professional Development Degree is an unusual one, clearly beyond Bachelor's level, perhaps roughly equivalent to a Master's.

Students select the courses, time, format, and place and may pace the study to complete the program from within one to seven years. A guided, independent study project is required.

A Bachelor of Science in engineering, or equivalent degree, is required for admission to the program. The average P.D.D. program costs between $2500 and $4500 depending on the courses selected. Correspondence courses are the most cost-effective method of completing the course requirements.

Upper Iowa University

Accredited Bachelor's degree in business subjects by home study with one or two weeks on campus in Iowa.

External Degree Program
P.O. Box 1861
Fayette, IA 52142

Telephone: (319) 425-5251
Fax: (319) 425-5271

Toll-free phone: (800) 553-4150
Year established: 1857

Degree levels: Bachelor's
Key person: Dave Fritz
Accreditation: Accredited
Ownership status: Nonprofit, independent
Residency: Short residency
Cost index: $$

Fields of study or special interest:
Accounting, management, marketing, public administration

Other information:
Upper Iowa's External Degree Program offers the opportunity to earn a Bachelor of Science degree in accounting, management, marketing, or public administration with one course taken in residency for one or two weeks. The balance of the program is conducted through directed independent study, with learning courses containing assignments and other course materials. Lessons may be faxed.

Frequent interaction with the faculty is encouraged by phone or mail.

A two-week summer session offered on the Fayette campus allows students to complete six semester hours of credit. Home study courses are available in a wide variety of fields, from accounting to chemistry, history to fine arts. Previous college work, job training, and other educational experience is evaluated for credit. Military credit is transcripted as recommended by the American Council of Education Military Evaluation Guide.

Walden University

Accredited Doctorates in education and management, requiring one three-week summer session in Indiana plus a few short local weekends.

415 First Avenue North
Minneapolis, MN 55401

Telephone: (612) 338-7224
Fax: (612) 338-5092

Toll-free phone: (800) 444-6795
Year established: 1970

Degree levels: Doctorate
Key person: Dr. Glendon Drake
Accreditation: Accredited
Ownership status: Nonprofit, independent
Residency: Short residency
Cost index: $$$$

Fields of study or special interest:
Administration/management, education, human services, health services

Other information:
Walden serves midcareer professionals with a Master's or equivalent. Doctoral programs (Ed.D. or Ph.D.) can be completed through a combination of independent study, intensive weekend sessions held regionally, personal interaction with the faculty, and a three-week summer residency at Indiana University.

Admissions workshops are held in a dozen or more cities in the U.S. and Canada each year. Each student is guided by a faculty advisor, with a reader and external consultant/examiner added at the dissertation stage. Each student completes a series of knowledge area modules, in areas ranging from research methodology to social systems. Ed.D. candidates must complete a 200-hour supervised internship.

Walden received its accreditation in 1990. The academic policy board is chaired by Harold Hodgkinson, former director of the National Institutes of Education.

Washington School of Law

Unaccredited nonresident Master's and Doctorates in taxation for CPAs, lawyers, and other businesspeople.

Washington Institute for Graduate Studies
2268 E. Newcastle Dr.
Sandy (Salt Lake City), UT 84093

Telephone: (801) 943-2440
Fax: ——

Toll-free:——
Year established: 1986

Degree levels: Master's, Doctorate
Key person: Gary James Joslin
Accreditation: Unaccredited
Ownership status: Nonprofit, independent
Residency: Nonresident
Cost index: $$$

Fields of study or special interest:
Taxation

Other information:
Lawyers and CPAs may earn the Master's degree in taxation (LL.M. Tax for lawyers, M.S. Tax for CPAs). three hundred sixty hours of class is required, in residence or through home-study videotapes. Most students take two years to complete the program. The college uses what they identify as the most advanced integrated system of textbooks on taxation of any graduate tax program.

The doctorate (J.S.D. for lawyers, Ph.D. for CPAs) requires the Master's in taxation, and a book-length dissertation of publishable quality, which must be defended before a panel of specialists.

The school is accepted for CPE credit by the Treasury, Internal Revenue Service for Enrolled Agents, the National Association of State Boards of Accountancy, and by the state boards of accountancy of virtually all states requiring such approval. The college is a division of Washington Institute for Graduate Studies, a Utah educational corporation. Accreditation is from the Accrediting Commission for Higher Education of the National Association of Private Nontraditional Schools and Colleges, a legitimate but unrecognized accrediting agency which is applying for recognition from the Department of Education.

Weber State University

Accredited Associate's and Bachelor's degrees in allied health sciences entirely through nonresident independent study.

Office of College of Health Professions Outreach Program
Ogden, UT 84408

Telephone: (801) 626-7164

Fax: (801) 626-7922

Toll-free phone: (800) 848-7770, ext.7164

Year established: 1889

Degree levels: Associate's, Bachelor's
Key person: William E. Smith
Accreditation: Accredited
Ownership status: Nonprofit, state
Residency: Short residency
Cost index: $$

Fields of study or special interest:
Allied health sciences

Other information:
Bachelor of Science in allied health sciences degree with majors/primary emphases in health administrative services, advanced radiological sciences, respiratory therapy, and advanced dental hygiene. There are also secondary emphases (minors). Credit is given for equivalency exams and military experience. At least 45 credit hours must be taken through WSU.

The program is delivered through independent study and intensive study. Correspondence courses include textbooks, study guides, modules, video- and audiotapes, and other learning aids prepared by the instructor. The student is assigned an instructor for each course, and keeps contact through phone and mail. The student has up to six months to complete each course.

Study-intensive workshop sessions are offered. Sessions are held either through attendance at four three- or four-day sessions per year at various sites (Billings, MT, Seattle, WA) or at two six-day "super sessions" at Weber State. The number of intensive courses to be taken depends on the student's primary and secondary emphases.

Western Illinois University

Accredited nonresident Bachelor's degree in many fields of study entirely through home study.

Non-Traditional Programs
5 Horrubin Hall
Macomb, IL 61455

Telephone: (309) 298-1929
Fax: (309) 298-2400

Toll-free phone:——
Year established: 1899

Degree levels: Bachelor's
Key person: Dr. Hans Moll
Accreditation: Accredited
Ownership status: Nonprofit, state
Residency: Nonresident
Cost index: $$

Fields of study or special interest:
Many fields

Other information:
The Board of Governors (BOG) B.A. can be earned entirely by correspondence study. Fifteen of 120 semester hours must be earned through one or a combination of BOG Universities, and 40 must be upper division. The 15 units that must be earned through enrollment at a BOG University can be done by correspondence, on campus in Macomb, or through extension courses at locations around the state.

Students who did not graduate from an Illinois high school must pass an exam on the U.S. and Illinois state constitution, or take an equivalent course in political science. All students must pass a university writing exam.

Western Illinois provides a helpful guide to the preparation of a prior learning portfolio. Credit for learning experiences and many equivalency exams. The total cost of the program depends on the number and type of courses taken. The cost of assessing a life experience portfolio is only $30.

Students from other countries are admitted, but they must have a U.S. address to which materials can be sent.

Appendices

Appendix A

For More Information on Schools in This Book

IF YOU HAVE QUESTIONS about one of the hundred schools described in this book, don't hesitate to write to me. I'll do my best to help. These are the ground rules:

What to do before writing to me

◆ Do your homework. Check with your local library or the relevant state education department or the Better Business Bureau before writing to me.

◆ Schools do move, and the Post Office will only forward mail for a short while. If a letter comes back as "undeliverable," then call Directory Assistance ("Information") in their city and see if they have a phone.

◆ Schools do change their phone numbers, and the telephone companies will only notify you of the new number for a short while. If you can't reach a school by phone, write them or try Information in their city to see if there has been a change.

Writing to me

◆ If you cannot reach them by phone or mail . . . or if you have new information you think I should know . . . or if you have questions or problems, then please write to let me know. I may be able to help.

◆ Enclose a self-addressed stamped envelope. If you are outside the U.S., enclose two International Postal Reply Coupons, available at your post office.

◆ If you want extensive advice or opinions on your personal situation, you will need to use the Degree Consulting Service which I established (although I no longer run it), which is described in Appendix C.

◆ Don't get too annoyed if I don't respond promptly. I do my best, but I get overwhelmed sometimes, and I travel a lot.

◆ Please don't telephone.

◆ Write to me thus:

Dr. John Bear,
P.O. Box 7070
Berkeley, California 94707 U.S.A.

Appendix B

For Information on Schools **Not** in This Book

THERE ARE TWO REASONS WHY a school in which you might be interested is not described in this book.

- ◆ It might have been relevant, but I chose not to make it one of the hundred described schools.
- ◆ It is not relevant for this book, since it does not offer degrees entirely or mostly by home study.

If you have questions about a school that is not described in this book, here is what I would suggest, in the following order:

1. Check Appendix D, where I have listed dozens of schools that offer degrees by home study—good, bad, and otherwise—that are *not* described in this book. It might be there.

2. Look it up in one of the standard school directories which you should find in any public library or bookstore: Lovejoy's, Barron's, Peterson's, Patterson's, ARCO, Cass & Birnbaum, and half a dozen others. Those books describe virtually every traditional college and university in the U.S. and Canada.

3. Ask for the help of a reference librarian. Your tax dollars pay their salaries.

4. If you know the location of the school, even the state, check with the relevant state education agency.

5. It will very likely be described in another book I have written, which has shorter descriptions of more than 500 nontraditional programs, as well as brief descriptions of more than 200 phony schools and diploma mills. That book is called *Bear's Guide to Earning College Degrees Nontraditionally*. For information on it, write to C&B Publishers, P.O. Box 826-T, Benecia, CA 94510, or call (800) 835-8535. You will be sent a free 16-page booklet telling all about this other book.

If none of the above approaches produce any useful information, then write to me and I will do what I can to help.

- ◆ Enclose a self-addressed stamped envelope.
- ◆ If you want extensive advice or opinions on your personal situation, you will need to use the Degree Consulting Service which I established (although I no longer run it), which is described in Appendix C.
- ◆ Don't get too annoyed if I don't respond promptly. I do my best, but I get overwhelmed sometimes, and I travel a lot.
- ◆ Please don't telephone.
- ◆ Write to me thus:

Dr. John Bear
P.O. Box 7070
Berkeley, California 94707 USA

Appendix C

For Personal Advice on Your Own Situation

IF YOU WOULD LIKE personal advice and recommendations, based on your own specific situation, a personal counseling service is available, by mail. I started this service in 1977, at the request of many readers. The actual personal evaluations and consulting are done by two friends and colleagues of mine, who are leading experts in the field of nontraditional education.

For a modest consulting fee, these things are done:

1. You will get a long personal letter (usually four to six typewritten pages) evaluating your situation, recommending the best degree programs for you (including part-time programs in your area) and estimating how long it will take and what it will cost you to complete your degree(s).

2. You will get answers to any specific questions you may have, with regard to any programs you may now be considering, institutions you have already dealt with, or other relevant matters.

3. You will get detailed, up-to-the-minute information on institutions and degree programs, equivalency exams, sources of the correspondence courses you may need, career opportunities, resumé writing, sources of financial aid, and other topics, in the form of prepared notes (some thirty pages of these) and a large sixteen-page booklet.

4. You will be able to telephone or write the service, to get as much follow-up counseling as you want, to keep updated on new programs and other changes, and to use the service as your personal information resource.

If you are interested in this personal counseling, please write or call and you will be sent descriptive literature and a counseling questionnaire, without cost or obligation.

Once you have these materials, if you wish counseling, simply fill out the questionnaire and return it, with a letter and resume if you like, along with the fee, and your personal reply and counseling materials will be airmailed to you.

For free information, write or telephone:

Degree Consulting Services
P. O. Box 3533
Santa Rosa, California 95402
(707) 539-6466

NOTE: Use this address only to reach the counseling service. For all other matters, please write to me at P.O. Box 7070, Berkeley, California 94707. Thank you.

Appendix D

Some Schools that are Not in This Book

THERE ARE MORE THAN 5,000 degree-granting colleges and universities on this planet, which means that more than 4,900 have not been included in this book: most because they do not offer relevant degree programs; some because they are terrible places that you don't want to deal with, and some because there just wasn't room for everyone and some schools had to be left out. Here are brief descriptions of some degree-granting institutions that were not included, along with my reasons for exclusion. I am putting these in because they are schools I am often asked about. Some are excellent, some are terrible, some are in between.

AMERICAN HOLISTIC COLLEGE OF NUTRITION, Alabama
See Chadwick University

AMERICAN INSTITUTE OF COMPUTER SCIENCES, Alabama
See Chadwick University

AMERICAN INTERNATIONAL UNIVERSITY, California
Diploma mill established by Edward Reddeck, who was later to move on to the equally phony University of North America.

AMERICAN NATIONAL UNIVERSITY, California
Major diploma mill that operated worldwide in the 70s and 80s.

ANDREW JACKSON UNIVERSITY or COLLEGE, Maryland
Unaccredited school established in Louisiana by Dr. Jean-Maximillien De La Croix de Lafayette, lawyer, author, and art patron; later moved to Maryland; now apparently dormant.

ANGLO-AMERICAN INSTITUTE OF DRUGLESS THERAPY, Scotland
Unaccredited nonresident Doctorates in naturopathy.

BARD COLLEGE, New York
A short-residency Bachelor's degree designed "to meet the special needs of adults who have left college . . ." Students meet with tutors twice a month.

BEREAN COLLEGE, Missouri
Accredited nonresident Bachelor's degrees in religious subjects.

BERNADEAN UNIVERSITY, California
Correspondence law and other degrees. For a time, offered a certificate good for absolution of all sins with each degree.

CALIFORNIA PACIFICA UNIVERSITY, California
Major diploma mill exposed by 60 Minutes; the proprietor went to prison.

CALIFORNIA UNIVERSITY FOR ADVANCED STUDIES, California
One of California's larger nonresident universities lost their license to operate and went out of business in the early 1990s.

CANADIAN SCHOOL OF MANAGEMENT, Canada
Legitimate formerly accredited school offering home study training in business.

CENTURY UNIVERSITY, New Mexico
Nonresident school, formerly in California. Accreditation is claimed from an unrecognized agency.

CHADWICK UNIVERSITY, Alabama
Dr. Lloyd Clayton operates four institutions of higher learning in Birmingham. They have nearly identical small catalogues that do not mention faculty or staff. The programs are all inexpensive and not excessively arduous. Dr. Clayton has been invited to stop accepting students by the state of Alabama, but this does not affect his out-of-state operations.

CITY UNIVERSITY LOS ANGELES, California
Unaccredited nonresident school offering degrees at all levels, including law.

CLAYTON UNIVERSITY, Missouri
In previous books, I have said positive things about Clayton. They have now apparently ceased operations in the U.S., and seem to be focusing on enrolling students from other countries only.

COAST UNIVERSITY, Hawaii
A diploma mill operated by Edward Reddeck until 1992 when he was exposed on *Inside Edition*. He was then indicted by a Federal Grand Jury and, in March 1993, convicted of 22 counts of fraud. Also known as Gold Coast University, North American University, and University of North America.

COLUMBIA UNIVERSITY, New York
They have an innovative Doctor of Education program called AEGIS (Adult Education Guided Independent Study), which can be earned by attending seminars one weekend day a month for two years plus a three-week summer intensive.

COLUMBIA STATE UNIVERSITY, Louisiana and Hawaii
The address is a mail forwarding service which sends the mail to a man named Ronald Tellar in Huntington Beach, California. Neither the accreditation claims nor the claims that various famous people have degrees from this school are true. Using the name "Herald Crenshaw," Mr. Tellar has published a book similar in appearance and title to this one, in which Columbia State University is identified as the "best university in America," and very unkind things are said about yours truly.

DARTMOUTH COLLEGE, New Hampshire
They have an M.A. in liberal studies which can be earned by attending for three consecutive summers.

DYKE COLLEGE, Ohio
Very short residency Bachelor's degrees for people living in or near Cleveland.

EULA WESLEY UNIVERSITY, Louisiana
They are really in Arizona, where the Phoenix newspaper reported that the founder, Dr. Samuel Wesley, runs things from his home. Dr. Wesley's Doctorate is from Eula Wesley University.

EUROTECHNICAL RESEARCH UNIVERSITY, Hawaii
Once a reputable unaccredited California school offering respectable advanced degrees in the sciences, the school moved to Hawaii and became involved with an Ohio karate school, Rockwell College, operated by a man whose only degrees were two doctorates purchased from the Universal Life Church. E.R.U. operates from two small rooms in the home of its president, Professor James Holbrook. It offers nonresident Doctorates in martial arts. A flagrant diploma mill named Leiland College operates from a Hawaii post office box originally opened by Professor Holbrook (who denies any connection or involvement with Leiland).

FAIRFAX UNIVERSITY, Louisiana
The premises are a secretarial service which forwards mail and messages to England. I have had numerous complaints from students regarding, among other things, the difficulty of reaching people. (The University announced, for instance, that it would close down entirely, no mail or phone calls or visits, for two of the last five months of 1990.) My wife and I were two of the four founders, but we resigned about two months after the first students enrolled in 1986. Although I thought we had parted company amicably, within weeks President Alan Jones was attempting (unsuccessfully) to get authorities in California to enjoin me from selling my book on earning degrees, because he did not like certain things I said in it about one of Fairfax's competitors.

GOLD COAST UNIVERSITY, Hawaii
See: Coast University, this section.

HARVARD UNIVERSITY, Massachusetts
You can actually do half a Harvard Bachelor's degree by correspondence, then spend two years there and get a Bachelor of Liberal Arts.

HONOLULU UNIVERSITY OF ARTS AND SCIENCES AND MANAGEMENT, Hawaii
Unaccredited nonresident school, originally established as Golden State University in California.

INTERNATIONAL INSTITUTE FOR ADVANCED STUDIES, Missouri
The degree programs are now part of Greenwich University, which is described in this book.

INTERNATIONAL UNIVERSITY, Missouri
Claims offices all over the world; claims accreditation from an unrecognized agency; no faculty listed in catalog.

INTERNATIONAL UNIVERSITY, New York
They claim to operate from island of St. Kitts, but apparently actually do so from New York, and have never responded to my many letters.

INTERNATIONAL UNIVERSITY FOR NUTRITION EDUCATION, California
Formerly Donsbach University, offering nonresident degrees in nutritional areas.

KENSINGTON UNIVERSITY, California
Unaccredited nonresident school, long established in California. The president is an attorney, and the school has had some good success in having graduates pass the California bar exam.

KENT COLLEGE, Louisiana
Same management as La Salle University.

KNIGHTSBRIDGE UNIVERSITY, Denmark and England
A nonexistent but heavily advertised new "university," established by the same man who used to run the equally nonexistent University de la Romande. The mailing address is in Denmark, but the school is run from England.

LA SALLE UNIVERSITY, Louisiana
As a purely religious school, not relevant for this book. The literature states that "the Biblical Christian perspective serves as the framework and intertwining basis for the conduct of all educational programs at LaSalle."All programs are offered through the education ministry of the World Christian Church, and are denominational, theocentric, and nonsecular. Acceptance as a student is acceptance into the church's education ministry.

LEILAND COLLEGE OF ARTS AND SCIENCES, Hawaii
See: Eurotechnical Research University in this section.

LONDON SCHOOL FOR SOCIAL RESEARCH, London
Nonexistent school that resurfaces from time to time, selling fake degrees.

LOUISIANA PACIFIC UNIVERSITY, Louisiana
The address is a secretarial service.

METROPOLITAN STATE UNIVERSITY, Minnesota
Very short residency degrees, primarily for Minnesotans.

NORTH AMERICAN UNIVERSITY, Utah, Washington, Missouri and Hawaii
A notorious diploma mill, run by Edward Reddeck, who had previously served time in prison for educational scams. This one was started in Missouri, where it was shut down by the Attorney General and fined $2,500,000. He fled to Utah, then to Hawaii, which took no action against him. The "school" name was changed to Gold Coast University, then Coast University. He was finally arrested by federal authorities and imprisoned again.

PACIFIC SOUTHERN UNIVERSITY
Unaccredited school offering degrees entirely through home study.

PACIFIC WESTERN UNIVERSITY
Unaccredited school offering degrees entirely through home study.

REID COLLEGE OF DETECTION OF DECEPTION, Illinois
Unaccredited Master's in polygraph use, based on a six-month course.

ROCKWELL COLLEGE OF ARTS AND SCIENCES
See: Eurotechnical Research University in this chapter.

SAINT JOHN'S UNIVERSITY, Louisiana

Run from the President's home, they offer a wide range of degrees by correspondence and do not ask too much of their students.

SOMERSET UNIVERSITY, Louisiana and England

The Louisiana address is a mail forwarding service. President Raymond Young formerly operated the no-longer-operating Harley College and St. Giles University College in England.

SOUTHWESTERN UNIVERSITY, Arizona

Major diploma mill operating in the 80s; the proprietor was sent to prison.

SUSSEX COLLEGE OF TECHNOLOGY, England

A well-known British degree mill which advertises extensively in the U.S. and elsewhere. Some people do some work for the degrees, but others just pay the fee for whatever they want. When the law required them to stop offering degrees to people who applied after a certain date, they simply began back-dating the applications, and roll merrily along.

THEOLOGICAL UNIVERSITY OF AMERICA, Louisiana

See University of America.

UNIVERSAL LIFE UNIVERSITY, California

Run by the Universal Life Church; an offering of up to $100 gets you the degree of your choice.

UNIVERSITY DE LA ROMANDE, England

A nonexistent English school that once claimed to be a fully-accredited Swiss school. See Knightsbridge University, this section.

UNIVERSITY OF AMERICA, Louisiana

The same management as the Theological University of America; the catalogs are identical but for a few religious references in the latter. The listed faculty have good credentials. The address is a secretarial service.

UNIVERSITY OF BEVERLY HILLS, Iowa

They tell authorities they are no longer operating, but they continue to advertise in Spain, Malaysia, and elsewhere.

UNIVERSITY OF EAST GEORGIA, Georgia

Phony school whose owner was nabbed by the FBI and sent to prison.

UNIVERSITY OF ENGLAND, Oxford

Nonexistent but heavily advertised school; I had the pleasure of testifying against their founders, five of whom went to prison in 1989.

UNIVERSITY OF NORTH AMERICA, Missouri

The former name of the diploma mill now called North American University. They advertised widely in USA Today and other national publications and sold degrees to a great many people, some of them willing co-conspirators and some actually believing they had earned the degree from a reputable school.

UNIVERSITY OF SANTA MONICA, California

Unaccredited but reputable state-licensed school, formerly Koh-E-Nor University.

VILLARREAL NATIONAL UNIVERSITY, Peru

The university is large and legitimate, but their distance learning degrees, in English, aroused much concern in the US as to their legitimacy, whether they were sanctioned by the university itself, and various aspects of their representation outside of Peru. There were three separate U.S. offices over a period of four years (in Georgia, Louisiana and California), and now an affiliation with the unaccredited Somerset University whose address is a secretarial service in New Orleans.

WESTERN STATES UNIVERSITY

They apparently operate legally in Missouri and in the Philippines, offering nonresident degrees, but their founder has two totally phony degrees of his own.

WILLIAM LYON UNIVERSITY, California

Unaccredited but state-approved degrees at all levels, with no visits to campus, but in-person meetings with faculty mentors.

WORLD UNIVERSITY OF AMERICA, California

Unaccredited, but state approved, with opportunity to earn degrees in astrology, out of body experience, avasthology, and spiritual ministry.

Appendix E
State Laws in Transition

LAWS ARE RARELY CARVED IN STONE. Both laws and the interpretation of the laws can change. This is certainly true in the area of school recognition and acceptance of degrees. Many nontraditional schools and most unaccredited schools are located in one of four states: California, Florida, Hawaii, or Louisiana. And the situation in each state is in flux, due to new laws, or new interpretations, or both.

Often, laws are quite imprecise. For instance, a school licensing law may say, "The State Department of Education shall establish standards and procedures for licensing degree-granting schools, and implement them by" such and such a date. Then it is up to state officials to make the policies. And even then, laws are always subject to challenge by people who don't like them (or are arrested for violation of them), and sometimes the laws (and the policies that implement them) are revised or even overturned by the legal system. Here is the situation in the four states with the most nontraditional schools:

California

In 1989, the state of California, following a series of editorials in major newspapers, passed a new Higher Education Act. Some of it was quite precise, such as the provision eliminating the category of "State Authorized" schools (and thereby sending quite a few schools heading for other states, or out of business). Some of it directed that a new state regulatory agency be established, which in turn would determine policies and procedures for evaluating and licensing schools. This process has moved slowly along. Some State Department of Education officials have sent up trial balloons on policy matters ("No more Doctorates through home study," "No more degrees in psychology," "All degree programs at least one year long," etc.), but many were shot down. Insiders have told me that many processes in Sacramento slowed down after the state's highest education official, the Superintendent of Public Instruction, was indicted on various felony charges. His conviction on all counts in February 1993 is unlikely to speed anything up.

Florida

Florida used to encourage legitimate unaccredited schools to operate, and had a special licensing procedure for them. Then, a couple of years ago, the pendulum swung totally in the other direction, and now Florida has quite a strange and repressive law. Unaccredited schools are apparently allowed to operate in the state, but it is a crime to use an unaccredited degree in any way whatsoever, even on a business card or letterhead. And there is no "grandfather" clause, so people who earned completely legal degrees from Florida-licensed unaccredited schools are now considered criminals if they tell anyone they have such a degree. As of the spring of 1993, a challenge to this law was working its way through the courts.

Hawaii

For many years, Hawaii was known as a state that had no laws at all regulating or licensing colleges or universities. In 1990, following testimony by various public citizens and experts (I was one of them), the legislature passed and the governor signed a law requiring the state Department of Consumer Protection to establish a school licensing or registration procedure. But three years later, the state had not established procedures, nor had they begun to implement the new law. This is very slow, even for Hawaii. More and more schools, good, bad and totally illegal, have been moving to Hawaii (or at least using convenience addresses there).

Louisiana

For many years, the only requirement for operating a school in Louisiana was to fill out a short, simple form, and file it with the Board of Regents, which had no power whatever to reject it. The Board of Regents did make clear that no school could say or imply that they were "approved" by or "recognized" by the state. This regulation has frequently been broken. During the 1980s and early 1990s, Louisiana became the home of more than fifty unaccredited colleges and universities, some of them good, many of them bad, and a few of them totally fraudulent diploma mills. But then, in 1992 the Louisiana legislature passed a law giving more power to the Board of Regents to regulate schools. This new law is slowly being interpreted and applied. It looks as if any "school" that does not have an actual physical presence in the state will no longer be registered. At least half a dozen have already "moved" from a Louisiana secretarial service to a Hawaii secretarial service, and others are likely to follow.

Appendix F

Bending the Rules

ONE OF THE MOST COMMON COMPLAINTS or admonishments I get from readers takes the form of "You said thus-and-so, but when I inquired of the school, they told me such-and-such." Often, a school claims that a program I have written about does not exist. Sometimes a student achieves something (such as completing a certain degree entirely by correspondence) that I had been told by a high official of the school was impossible.

One of the open "secrets" in the world of higher education is that the rules are constantly being bent. But, like the Emperor's new clothes, no one dares point and say what is really going on, especially in print.

The purpose of this brief essay is to acknowledge that this sort of thing happens all the time. If you know that it happens regularly, then at least you are in the same boat with people who are benefiting already by virtue of bent rules.

Unfortunately, I cannot provide many specific examples of bent rules, naming names and all. This is for two good reasons:

1. Many situations where students profit from bent rules would disappear in an instant if anyone dared mention the situation publicly. There is, for instance, a major state university that is forbidden by its charter from granting degrees for correspondence study. But they regularly work out special arrangements for students, who are carried on the books as residential students, even though all work is done by mail, and some of the graduates have never set foot on the campus. If this ever "got out," the Board of Trustees, the accrediting agency, and all the other universities in that state would probably have conniptions, and the practice would be suspended at once.

2. These kinds of things can change so rapidly, with new personnel or new policies, that a listing of anomalies and curious practices would probably be obsolete before the ink dried.

Consider a few examples of the sort of thing that is going on in higher education every day, whether or not anyone will admit it, except perhaps behind closed doors or after several drinks:

◆ A friend of mine, at a major university, was unable to complete one required course for her Doctorate, before she had to leave for another state. This university does not offer correspondence courses, but she was able to convince a professor to enroll her in a regular course, which she would just "happen" never to visit in person.

◆ A man in graduate school needed to be enrolled in nine units of coursework each semester to keep his employer's tuition assistance plan going. But his job was too demanding one year, and he was unable to do so. The school enrolled him in nine units of "independent study" for which no work was asked or required, and for which a "pass" grade was given.

◆ A woman at a large school needed to get a certain number of units before an inflexible time deadline. When it was clear she was not going to make it, a kindly professor turned in grades for her, and told her she could do the actual coursework later on.

◆ A major state university offers nonresident degrees for people living in that state only. When a reader wrote me to say that he, living a thousand miles from that state, was able to complete his degree entirely by correspondence, I asked a contact at that school what was going on. "We will take students from anywhere in our correspondence degree program," she told me, "But for God's sake, don't print that in your book, or we'll be deluged with applicants."

◆ If we are to believe a book by a member of Dr. Bill Cosby's dissertation committee at the University of Massachusetts (*Education's Smoking Gun* by Reginald Damerell), the only class attendance on Cosby's transcript was one weekend seminar, and the only dissertation committee meeting was a dinner party, with spouses, at Cosby's house.

◆ Part way through my final doctoral oral exam, a key member of my committee had to leave for an emergency. He scrawled a note, and passed it to the Dean who read it, then crumpled it up and threw it away. The grueling exam continued for several hours more. After it was over and the committee had congratulated me and departed, I retrieved the note from the wastebasket. It read, "Please give John my apologies for having to leave, and my congratulations for having passed."

◆ A man applied to a well-known school that has a rigid requirement that all graduate work (thesis or dissertation) must be begun after enrollment. He started to tell an admissions officer about a major piece of independent research he had completed for his employer. "Stop," he was told, "Don't tell me about that. Then you will be able to use it for your Master's thesis."

◆ My eldest daughter was denied admission to the University of California at Berkeley because of some "irregularities" on her high school transcript. (It was a nontraditional high school.) The high school's records had been destroyed in a fire. The former principal checked with the University, discovered that the admissions people would be glad to admit her, once the computer said it was okay. He typed up a new transcript saying what the computer wanted said. The computer said okay, and three years later, said daughter graduated Phi Beta Kappa. But how many other applicants accepted the initial "No," not knowing that rules can often be bent?

Please use this information prudently. It will probably do no good to pound on a table and say, "What do you mean I can't do this? John Bear says that rules don't mean anything, anyway."

But when faced with a problem, it surely can do no harm to remember that there do exist many situations in which the rules have turned out to be far less rigid than the printed literature of a school would lead one to believe.

Appendix G

Advice for People in Prison

NOTE: *More than a few readers and users of this book are people who are institutionalized, or friends and relatives of those who are. For this edition, I have invited a man who has completed his Bachelor's and Master's from prison, and who consults often with inmates and others around the country, to offer his thoughts and recommendations. There is some very useful advice for non-institutionalized persons as well.*

Arranging Academic Resources for the Institutionalized

by Douglas G. Dean

One obstacle for any institutionalized person interested in pursuing a degree is limited resources: availability of community faculty, library facilities, phone access, and financial aid. To overcome these, it helps to streamline the matriculation process. Time spent in preparation prior to admission can help avoid wasted effort and time when in a program, thereby reducing operating expenses and cutting down the number of tuition periods.

A second obstacle is finding ways to ensure that a quality education can be documented. Because courses are generally not prepackaged, it is the student's responsibility to identify varied learning settings, use varied learning methods, find and recruit community-based faculty, provide objective means to appraise what has been learned, and indeed design the study plan itself.

Find a flexible degree program

Most well-established degree programs grant credit for a variety of learning experiences. In terms of cost and arrangements required, equivalency examinations and independent study projects are the most expedient. Credit for life experience learning is another option sometimes offered. If a degree program does not offer at least these first two options, it is unlikely that the program as a whole will be able to accommodate the needs of the institutionalized student.

Write a competency-based study plan

The traditional method of acquiring credits is to take narrowly focused courses of two to four credits each. Since the nontraditional student must enlist his or her own instructors, find varied learning methods, and quantify the whole experience, the single course approach creates much needless duplication of effort.

A better approach is to envision a subject area which is to be studied for nine to twelve credits (e.g., statistics). As an independent study project, the student identifies what topics are germane to the area (e.g., probability theory, descriptive statistics, inferential statistics); at what level of comprehension (e.g., introductory through intermediate or advanced); how the topic is to be studied (e.g., directed reading, programmed textbooks), and how the competencies acquired are to be demonstrated (e.g., oral examination, proctored examination including problem solving). This way, a single independent study project can take the place of a series of successive courses in a given area (e.g., statistics 101, 201, 301).

Designing the curriculum

Every accredited degree program has graduation requirements. These requirements broadly define the breadth of subject areas that comprise a liberal arts education and the depth to which they are to be studied. It is the responsibility of the external student not only to identify a curriculum fulfilling these requirements, but in most cases to design the course content that will comprise each study module.

But how does a student know what an area of study consists of before he or she has studied it? The answer lies in meticulous preparation.

Well in advance of formally applying for an off-campus degree program, the prospective student should obtain course catalogs from several colleges and universities. Look at what these schools consider the core curriculum, and what is necessary to fulfill the graduation requirements. With the broad outline in mind, the student can begin to form clusters of courses fulfilling each criterion. This helps shape the study plan academically rather than touch it up later as an afterthought.

Next, decide which subjects are of interest within each criterion area. Compare topical areas within each subject as described in the course listings, and commonalities will emerge. From there, it is simply a matter of writing to the various instructors for copies of their course syllabuses. These course outlines will provide more detailed information about the subject matter and identify the textbooks currently used at that level of study.

Means of study

Having decided what is to be studied, the student must then propose various ways to study it.

Equivalency exams enable the student to acquire credits instantly, often in core or required areas of study. This helps reduce overall program costs by eliminating the need for textbooks and tuition fees. More importantly, it helps reduce the number of special learning arrangements that must otherwise be made.

"Testing out" of correspondence courses (taking only the examinations, without doing the homework assignments) is another excellent way to acquire credits quickly. This can, however, be an expensive method since full course fees are still assessed. Nonetheless, if a student studies on his or her own in advance according to the course syllabus, and if the instructor can then be convinced to waive prerequisite assignments, it can be an efficient and cost-effective method to use.

Independent study projects should form the balance of any study plan. With the topical areas, learning objectives, and learning materials identified, an independent study project allows the student to remain with the same instructor(s) from an introductory through an intermediate or advanced level of study. This eliminates the need for new arrangements to be made every two to four credits. An independent study project can take the form of simple directed reading, tutorial instruction, practicum work, or a combination of these methods, culminating in the final product.

Independent study projects require the aid of qualified persons to act as community faculty, and to oversee personally the progress of the work. Therefore it is highly advantageous to line up faculty in advance of entering the degree program, and to have alternates available in the event an instructor is unable, for any reason, to fulfill his or her commitment. It is better to anticipate these needs at the preparatory stage than to be scrambling for a replacement while the tuition clock is running.

Multiple treatments of subject matter

The external student is without benefit of lecture halls, interactions with other students, or readily available academic counseling services. For the institutionalized student, picking up the phone or stopping in to see a faculty member for help with a study problem is not an option. This is why alternate methods of study are so valuable.

One approach is to use several textbooks covering the same subject matter. If something does not make sense, there is a different treatment of the subject to turn to.

Programmed textbooks make especially good substitute tutors. A programmed text breaks the subject matter into small segments requiring a response from the reader with periodic tests to check progress. Such texts are now available in many subject areas, but are particularly useful for the sciences. Titles can be learned from the subject guide to *Books in Print,* or by writing directly to textbook publishers.

Audio-visual materials can, to some extent, make up for college life without lectures and classes. Writing to A-V (audio-visual) departments at large universities often yields a catalog of materials available for rental. When using such materials, it is best to work through the school or social service department of the student's institution of residence.

Some large campuses have lecture note services, in which advanced students attend introductory lectures, and take copious lecture notes, which are then sold to students. Aside from their insights into good note-taking, these published notes are an additional treatment of course content. Such notes are especially recommended for new students.

Documenting study

The administrators of a degree program must be convinced that there are acceptable ways to document what has been learned, and what levels of subject mastery have been achieved, without taking the student's word for it. Community faculty members may be asked to provide written or oral examinations, but it does not hurt to make their jobs easier.

Most professions (accounting, psychology, law, medicine, etc.) have licensing and/or board certification examinations that must be taken. An industry has built up around this need, providing parallel or actual past examinations to help prepare students. By agreeing to take a relevant sample examination under proctored conditions, and negotiating a "pass" score in advance, the community faculty member is relieved of having to design his or her own objective examination for just one student. This approach adds validity to the assessment process, and provides a standardized score that has some universal meaning. This is an optional approach but may be worth the effort.

Recruiting community faculty

Just as it is easier for a student to organize a study plan in blocks of subject areas, a competency-based study plan of this sort makes it easier for a prospective instructor to visualize what is being asked of him or her.

A typical independent study project would define for the instructor what specific topics are to be studied, what levels of mastery will be expected of the student, what textbooks or other materials will be used, and what is expected of the instructor.

Many traditional academics are unfamiliar with external degree programs. Consequently, they tend to assume that their role as instructor will require greater effort and time on their part than for the average student, who may expect their services in many roles, from academic advisor to tutor. The more an institutionalized student can do up front to define clearly the role and expected duties of the community faculty member, the more successful a student will be in enlisting instructors for independent study projects.

Instructors may sometimes be found on the staff of the institution where the student resides. They may also be found through a canvas letter sent to the appropriate department heads at area colleges, universities, and technical schools. The same approach may be used to canvas departments within area businesses, museums, art centers, hospitals, libraries, theaters, zoos, banks, and orchestras, to name but a few. People are often flattered to be asked, providing it is clear to them exactly what they are getting into.

The more a student can operate independently, and rely on community faculty for little more than assessment purposes, the more likely a student will be successful in recruiting help, and thereby broadening the range of study options.

"Revealing" your institutionalized status

It is generally proper and appropriate to inform potential schools and potential faculty of one's institutionalized status. (Many institutions now have mailing addresses that do not indicate they are, in fact, institutions.) Some schools or individuals may be "put off" by this, but then you would not want to deal with them anyway. Others may be especially motivated to help.

Financing the educational process

Unfortunately, there are virtually no generalizations to be made here, whatsoever. Each institution seems to have its own policy with regard to the way finances are handled. Some institutionalized persons earn decent wages, and have access to the funds. Others have little or no ability to pay their own way. Some institutions permit financial gifts from relatives or friends, others do not. Some schools make special concessions or have some scholarship funds available for institutionalized persons; many do not. One should contact the financial aid office of the school to ask this question.

Some people have had success in approaching foundations for this purpose. One foundation that has specialized in helping incarcerated people pursue accredited degrees is the Davis-Putter Fund, 1820 Fleming Road, Louisville, KY 40205.

At the Bachelor's level, Ohio University offers degrees by correspondence study especially for people in prison, at significantly lower tuition than their usual programs.

In conclusion

Institutionalized students must be highly self-directed, and honest enough with themselves to recognize if they are not. Because the student lives where he or she works, it takes extra effort to set aside daily study time, not only to put the student in the right frame of mind, but also to accommodate institution schedules. It can mean working with a minimum number of books or tapes to comply with property rules. It means long periods of delayed gratification, in an environment where pursuing education is often suspect. And it is the greatest feeling in the world when it all comes together.

Appendix H
Glossary of Important Terms

academic year: The period of formal academic instruction, usually from September or October to May or June, divided into semesters, quarters, or trimesters.

accreditation: Recognition of a school by an independent private organization. Not a governmental function in the U.S. There are more than one hundred accrediting agencies, some recognized by the Department of Education and/or COPA, and some unrecognized, some phony or fraudulent.

ACT: American College Testing program, administrators of aptitude and achievement tests.

adjunct faculty: Part-time faculty member, often at a nontraditional school, often with a full-time teaching job elsewhere. More and more traditional schools are hiring adjunct faculty, because they don't have to pay them as much or provide health care and other benefits.

advanced placement: Admission to a school at a higher level than one would normally enter at, because of getting credit for prior learning experience or passing advanced placement exams.

alma mater: The school from which one has graduated, as in "My alma mater is Michigan State University."

alternative: Used interchangeably with *external* or *nontraditional*; offering an alternate, or different means of pursuing learning or degrees or both.

alumni: Graduates of a school, as in "This school has some distinguished alumni." The word is technically for males only; females are *alumnae*. The singular is *alumnus* (male) or *alumna* (female).

alumni association: A confederation of alumni and alumnae who have joined together to support their alma mater in various ways, generally by donating money.

approved: In California, a level of state recognition of a school, generally regarded as one step above *authorized* and one step below *accredited*.

arbitration: A means of settling disputes, as between a student and a school, in which one or more independent arbitrators or judges listen to both sides, and make a decision. A means of avoiding a courtroom trial. Many learning contracts have an arbitration clause. (See *binding arbitration, mediation.*)

assistantship: A means of assisting students (usually graduate students) financially by offering them part-time academic employment, usually in the form of a teaching assistantship or a research assistantship.

Associate's degree: A "two-year" degree, traditionally awarded by community or junior colleges after two years of residential study, or completion of 60 to 64 semester hours.

auditing: Sitting in on a class without earning credit for that class.

authorized: In California, a form of state recognition of schools, authorizing them to exist, to accept students, and to grant degrees.

Bachelor's degree: Awarded in the U.S. after four years of full-time residential study (two to five years in other countries), or earning from 120 to 124 semester units by any means.

binding arbitration: Arbitration in which both parties have agreed in advance that they will abide by the result and take no further legal action.

branch campus: A satellite facility, run by officers of the main campus of a college or university, at another location. Can range from a small office to a full-fledged university center.

campus: The main facility of a college or university, usually comprising buildings, grounds, dormitories, cafeterias and dining halls, sports stadia, etc. The campus of a nontraditional school may consist solely of offices.

chancellor: Often the highest official of a university. Also a new degree title, proposed by some schools, to be a higher degree than the Doctorate, and requiring three to five years of additional study.

CLEP: The College-Level Examination Program, a series of equivalency examinations given nationally each month.

coeducational: Education of men and women on the same campus or in the same program. This is why female students are called coeds.

college: In the U.S., an institution offering programs leading to the Associate's, Bachelor's, and possibly higher degrees. Often used interchangeably with *university* although traditionally a university is a collection of colleges. In England and elsewhere, *college* may denote part of a university (Kings College, Cambridge) or a private high school (Eton College).

colloquium: A gathering of scholars to discuss a given topic over a period of a few hours to a few days. ("The university is sponsoring a colloquium on marine biology.")

community college: A two-year traditional school, offering programs leading to the Associate's degree and, typically, many noncredit courses in arts, crafts, and vocational fields for community members not interested in a degree. Also called *junior college.*

competency: The philosophy and practice of awarding credit or degrees based on learning skills, rather than time spent in courses.

COPA: The Council on Postsecondary Accreditation, a private nongovernmental organization that recognizes accrediting agencies.

correspondence course: A course offered by mail, completed entirely by home study, often with one or two proctored, or supervised examinations.

course: A specific unit of instruction, such as a course in microeconomics, or a course in abnormal psychology. Residential courses last for one or more semesters or quarters; correspondence courses often have no rigid time requirements.

cramming: Intensive preparation for an examination. Most testing agencies now admit that cramming can improve scores on exams.

credit: Units used to record courses taken. Each credit typically represents the number of hours spent in class each week. Hence a three-credit or three-unit course would commonly be a class that met three hours each week for one semester or quarter.

curriculum: A program of courses to be taken in pursuit of a degree or other objective.

degree: A title conferred by a school to show that a certain course of study has been completed.

Department of Education: In the U.S., the national agency concerned with all educational matters not handled by the Departments of Education in the fifty states. In other countries, commonly the Ministry of Education.

diploma: The certificate that shows that a certain course of study has been completed. Diplomas are awarded for completing degree studies or other, shorter courses of study.

dissertation: The major research project normally required as part of the work for a Doctorate. Dissertations are expected to make a new and creative contribution to the field of study, or to demonstrate one's excellence in the field. (See also *thesis*.)

Doctorate: The highest degree one can earn (but see *chancellor*). Includes Doctor of Philosophy, Education, and many other titles.

dormitory: Student living quarters on residential campuses. May include dining halls and classrooms.

early decision: Making a decision on whether to admit a student sooner than decisions are usually made. Offered by some schools primarily as a service either to students applying to several schools, or those who are especially anxious to know the outcome of their application.

ECFMG: The Education Commission for Foreign Medical Graduates, which administers an examination to physicians who have gone to medical school outside the U.S. and wish to practice in the U.S.

electives: Courses one does not have to take, but may elect to take as part of a degree program.

essay test: An examination in which the student writes narrative sentences as answers to questions, instead of the short answers required by a multiple-choice test. Also called a *subjective test*.

equivalency examination: An examination designed to demonstrate knowledge in a subject where the learning was acquired outside a traditional classroom. A person who learned certain nursing skills while working in a hospital, for instance, could take an equivalency exam to earn credit in obstetrical nursing.

external: Away from the main campus or offices. An external degree may be earned by home study or at locations other than on the school's campus.

fees: Money paid to a school for purposes other than academic tuition. Fees might pay for parking, library services, use of the gymnasium, binding of dissertations, etc.

fellowship: A study grant, usually awarded to a graduate student, and usually requiring no work other than usual academic work (as contrasted with an *assistantship*).

financial aid: A catchall term, including scholarships, loans, fellowships, assistantships, tuition reductions, etc. Many schools have a financial aid officer.

fraternities: Men's fraternal and social organizations, often identified by Greek letters, such as Zeta Beta Tau. There are also professional and scholastic fraternities open to men and women, such as Beta Alpha Psi, the national fraternity for students of accounting.

freshman: The name for the class in its first of four years of traditional study for a Bachelor's degree, and its individual members. ("She is a freshman, and so is in the freshman class.")

grade point average: The average score a student has made in all his or her classes, weighted by the number of credits or units for each class. Also called G.P.A.

grades: Evaluative scores provided for each course, and often for individual examinations or papers written for that course. There are letter grades (usually A, B, C, D, F) and number grades (usually percentages from 0% to 100%), or on a scale of 0 to 3, 0 to 4, or 0 to 5. Some schools use a pass/fail system with no grades.

graduate: One who has earned a degree from a school, or the programs offered beyond the Bachelor's level. ("He is a graduate of Yale University, and is now working on his Master's in graduate school at Princeton.")

graduate school: A school or a division of a university offering work at the Master's or Doctoral degree level.

graduate student: One attending graduate school.

GRE: The Graduate Record Examination, which many traditional schools and a few non-traditional ones require for admission to graduate programs.

honor societies: Organizations for persons with a high grade point average or other evidence of outstanding performance. There are local societies on some campuses, and several national organizations, the most prestigious of which is called Phi Beta Kappa.

honor system: A system in which students are trusted not to cheat on examinations, and to obey other rules, without proctors or others monitoring their behavior.

honorary doctorate: A nonacademic award, given regularly by more than one thousand colleges and universities to honor distinguished scholars, celebrities, and donors of large sums of money. Holders of this award may, and often do, call themselves "Doctor."

junior: The name for the class in its third year of a traditional four-year U.S. Bachelor's degree program, or any member of that class. ("She is a junior this year, and is organizing the junior class prom.")

junior college: Same as *community college*.

language laboratory: A room with special audio equipment to facilitate learning languages by listening to tapes. Many students can be learning different languages at different skill levels at the same time.

learning contract: A formal agreement between a student and a school, specifying independent work to be done by the student, and the amount of credit the school will award on successful completion of the work.

lecture class: A course in which a faculty member lectures to anywhere from a few dozen to many hundreds of students. Often lecture classes are followed by small group discussion sessions led by student assistants or junior faculty.

liberal arts: A term with many complex meanings, but generally referring to the nonscientific curriculum of a university: humanities, the arts, social sciences, history, and so forth.

liberal education: Commonly taken to be the opposite of a specialized education; one in which students are required to take courses in a wide range of fields, as well as courses in their major.

licensed: Holding a permit to operate. This can range from a difficult-to-obtain state school license to a simple local business license.

life experience portfolio: A comprehensive presentation listing and describing all learning experiences in a person's life, with appropriate documentation. The basic document used in assigning academic credit for life experience learning.

LSAT: The Law School Admission Test, required by most U.S. law schools of all applicants.

maintenance costs: The expenses incurred while attending school, other than tuition and fees. Includes room and board (food), clothing, laundry, postage, travel, etc.

major: The subject or academic department in which a student takes concentrated coursework, leading to a specialty. ("His major is in English literature; she is majoring in chemistry.")

mentor: Faculty member assigned to supervise independent study work at a nontraditional school; comparable to *adjunct faculty*.

minor: The secondary subject or academic department in which a student takes concentrated coursework. ("She has a major in art and a minor in biology.")

MSAT: The Medical School Admission Test, required by most U.S. medical schools of all applicants.

multiple-choice test: An examination in which the student chooses the best of several alternative answers provided for each question; also called an *objective test*. ("The capital city of England is (a) London, (b) Ostrogotz-Plakatz, (c) Tokyo, (d) none of the above.")

multiversity: A university system with two or more separate campuses, each a major university in its own right, such as the University of California or the University of Wisconsin.

narrative transcript: A transcript issued by a nontraditional school in which, instead of simply listing the courses completed and grades received, there is a narrative description of the work done and the school's rationale for awarding credit for that work.

nontraditional: Something done in other than the usual or traditional way. In education, refers to learning and degrees completed by methods other than spending many hours in classrooms and lecture halls.

nonresident: (1) A means of instruction in which the student does not need to visit the school; all work is done by correspondence, telephone, or exchange of audio tapes or videotapes; (2) A person who does not meet residency requirements of a given school and, as a result, often has to pay a higher tuition or fees.

objective test: An examination in which questions requiring a very short answer are posed. It can be multiple choice, true-false, fill-in-the-blank, etc. The questions are related to facts (thus objective) rather than to opinions (or subjective).

on the job: In the U.S., experience or training gained through employment, which may be converted to academic credit. In England, slang for "having sex," which either confuses or amuses English people who read about "credit for on-the-job experience."

open admissions: An admissions policy in which everyone who applies is admitted, on the theory that the ones who are unable to do university work will drop out before long.

out-of-state student: One from a state other than that in which the school is located. Because most state colleges and universities have much higher tuition rates for out-of-state students, many people attempt to establish legal residence in the same state as their school.

parallel instruction: A method in which nonresident students do exactly the same work as residential students, during the same general time periods, except they do it at home.

pass/fail option: Instead of getting a letter or number grade in a course, the student may elect, at the start of the course, a pass/fail option in which the only grades are either "pass" or "fail." Some schools permit students to elect this option on one or two of their courses each semester.

PEP: Proficiency Examination Program, a series of equivalency exams given nationally every few months.

plan of study: A detailed description of the program an applicant to a school plans to pursue. Many traditional schools ask for this as part of the admissions procedure. The plan of study should be designed to meet the objectives of the *statement of purpose*.

portfolio: See *life experience portfolio*.

prerequisites: Courses that must be taken before certain other courses may be taken. For instance, a course in algebra is often a prerequisite for a course in geometry.

private school: A school that is privately owned, rather than operated by a governmental department.

proctor: A person who supervises the taking of an examination to be certain there is no cheating, and that other rules are followed. Many nontraditional schools permit unproctored examinations.

professional school: School in which one studies for the various professions, including medicine, dentistry, law, nursing, veterinary, optometry, ministry, etc.

PSAT: Preliminary Scholastic Aptitude Test, given annually to high-school juniors.

public school: In the U.S., a school operated by the government of a city, county, district, state, or the federal government. In England, a privately owned or run school.

quarter: An academic term at a school on the "quarter system," in which the calendar year is divided into four equal quarters. New courses begin each quarter.

quarter hour: An amount of credit earned for each classroom hour spent in a given course during a given quarter. A course that meets four hours each week for a quarter would probably be worth four quarter hours, or quarter units.

recognized: A term used by some schools to indicate approval from some other organization or governmental body. The term usually does not have a precise meaning, so it may mean different things in different places.

registrar: The official at most colleges and universities who is responsible for maintaining student records and, in many cases, for verifying and validating applications for admission.

rolling admissions: A year-round admissions procedure. Many schools only admit students once or twice a year. A school with rolling admissions considers each application at the time it is received. Many nontraditional schools, especially ones with nonresident programs, have rolling admissions.

SAT: Scholastic Aptitude Test, one of the standard tests given to qualify for admission to colleges and universities.

scholarship: A study grant, either in cash or in the form of tuition or fee reduction.

score: Numerical rating of performance on a test. ("His score on the Graduate Record Exam was not so good.")

semester: A school term, generally four to five months. Schools on the semester system will usually have two semesters a year, with a shorter summer session.

semester hour: An amount of credit earned in a course representing one classroom hour per week for a semester. A class that meets three days a week for one hour, or one day a week for three hours, would be worth three semester hours, or semester units.

seminar: A form of instruction combining independent research with meetings of small groups of students and a faculty member, generally to report on reading or research the students have done.

senior: The fourth year of study of a four-year U.S. Bachelor's degree program, or a member of that class. ("Linnea is a senior this year, and is president of the senior class.")

sophomore: The second year of study in a four-year U.S. Bachelor's degree program, or a member of that class.

sorority: A women's social organization, often with its own living quarters on or near a campus, and usually identified with two or three Greek letters, such as Sigma Chi.

special education: Education of the physically or mentally handicapped, or, often, of the gifted.

special student: A student who is not studying for a degree either because he or she is ineligible or does not wish the degree.

statement of purpose: A detailed description of the career the applicant intends to pursue after graduation. A statement of purpose is often requested as part of the admissions procedure at a university.

subject: An area of study or learning covering a single topic, such as the subject of chemistry, or economics, or French literature.

subjective test: An examination in which the answers are in the form of narrative sentences or long or short essays, often expressing opinions rather than reporting facts.

syllabus: A detailed description of a course of study, often including the books to be read, papers to be written, and examinations to be given.

thesis: The major piece of research that is completed by many Master's degree candidates. A thesis is expected to show a detailed knowledge of one's field and ability to do research and integrate knowledge of the field.

TOEFL: Test of English as a Foreign Language, required by many schools of persons for whom English is not their native language.

traditional education: Education at a residential school in which the Bachelor's degree is completed through four years of classroom study, the Master's in one or two years, and the Doctorate in three to five years.

transcript: A certified copy of the student's academic record, showing courses taken, examinations passed, credits awarded, and grades or scores received.

transfer student: A student who has earned credit in one school, and then transfers to another school.

trimester: A term consisting of one third of an academic year. Some schools have three equal trimesters each year.

tuition: In the U.S., the money charged for formal instruction. In some schools, tuition is the only expense other than postage. In other schools, there may be fees as well as tuition. In England, tuition refers to the instruction or teaching at a school, such as the tuition offered in history.

tuition waiver: A form of financial assistance in which the school charges little or no tuition.

tutor: See *mentor*. A tutor can also be a hired assistant who helps a student prepare for a given class or examination.

undergraduate: Pertaining to the period of study from the end of high school to the earning of a Bachelor's degree; also to a person in such a course of study. ("Barry is an undergraduate at Reed College, one of the leading undergraduate schools.")

university: An institution that usually comprises one or more undergraduate colleges, one or more graduate schools, and, often, one or more professional schools.

Index

University of Alabama, New College, 34, 144
University of Alaska, 34
University of America (Louisiana), 183
University of Arkansas, 35
University of Beverly Hills (Iowa), 183
University of California Extension, 35
University of Cincinnati, 115
University of Colorado, 35
University of Durham (England), 145
University of East Georgia, 183
University of England, 183
University of Florida, 35, 135
University of Georgia, 35
University of Idaho, 35, 147
University of Illinois, 35, 82
University of Iowa, 35, 148
University of Kansas, 35
University of Kentucky, 35
University of London (England), 149
University of Maryland, 106, 150
University College, 115
University of Massachusetts at Amherst, 151
University of Michigan, 35
University of Minnesota, 35, 152
University of Mississippi, 35
University of Missouri, 35
  at Columbia, 153
University of Nebraska, 36
University of Nevada, 36
University of New Mexico, 36
University of North America (Missouri), 182. *See also* North American University
University of North Carolina, 36, 43
University of North Dakota, 36
University of North Florida, 135
University of Northern Colorado, 36
University of Northern Iowa, 36, 148
University of Oklahoma, 36, 154
University of Phoenix (Arizona), 155
University of Santa Barbara (California), 156-57

University of Santa Monica (California), 183
University of Sarasota (Florida), 157
University of South Africa (UNISA), 158
University of South Carolina, 36
University of Southern Mississippi, 36
University of State of New York, 47, 82, 160
  Regents College, 42, 79
University of Tennessee, 36
University of Texas, 36
University of Utah, 37
University of Wales, 161
University of Warwick (England), 162
University of Washington, 37
University of Waterloo (Canada), 163
University of Wisconsin (Madison), 37, 164
University of Wyoming, 37
Upper Iowa University, 165
Utah, state accreditation agency for, 17
Utah State University, 37

Vermont, state accreditation agency for, 17
Villarreal National University (Peru), 184
Virginia, state accreditation agency for, 17
Volunteer work, as creditworthy life experience, 45

Walden University (Minnesota), 166
Washington, state accreditation agency for, 17
Washington Institute for Graduate Studies, (Utah), 167
Washington School of Law (Utah), 167
Washington State University, 37
Weber State University, 37, 168

Wesley, Dr. Samuel, 181
West European Accrediting Society, 28
West Virginia, state accreditation agency for, 17
Western Association of Private Alternative Schools, 28
Western Association of Schools and Colleges (Oakland), 26
Western Association of Schools and Colleges, 28
Western Council on Non-Traditional Private Post Secondary Education, 28
Western Illinois University, 37, 45, 115, 169
Western Michigan University, 37
Western Oregon State College, 37, 115
Western States University (Missouri), 27, 28, 184
Western Washington University, 37
William Lyon University (California), 184
Wisconsin, state accreditation agency for, 17
Women only, degrees offered to, 128
Work, as creditworthy life experience, 45
World Christian Church, 27
World Education Services, 52
World University of America (California), 184
Worldwide Accrediting Commission, 28
Wyoming, state accreditation agency for, 17

Xerox Corporation, credit for course offered by, 54

Y

Young, Raymond, 183